THOUGHT CATALOG BOOKS

# Love S.U.C.K.S.

# Love S.U.C.K.S.

## (Seems Unusually Confusing & Kinda Scary)

ISIS NEZBETH

THOUGHT CATALOG BOOKS

Brooklyn, NY

**THOUGHT CATALOG BOOKS**

Copyright © 2016 by Isis Nezbeth

All rights reserved. Published by Thought Catalog Books, a division of The Thought & Expression Co., Williamsburg, Brooklyn. Founded in 2010, Thought Catalog is a website and imprint dedicated to your ideas and stories. We publish fiction and non-fiction from emerging and established writers across all genres. For general information and submissions: manuscripts@thoughtcatalog.com.

First edition, 2016

ISBN 978-1945796005

10 9 8 7 6 5 4 3 2 1

Image © Patric Sandri / Offset.com, Design by KJ Parish

# Contents

1.  Why You Should Take Relationship Advice From Me — 1
2.  How To Slide In The Direct Messages — 5
3.  How To Talk To Someone You're Interested In On The Phone — 11
4.  4 Topics (Pretty Much) Anybody Loves To Talk About — 17
5.  3 Reasons To Go For The One Who Is Not Your Type — 21
6.  5 Reasons To Date Your Friend — 25
7.  15 Of The Sexiest Things Any Man Can Do — 29
8.  15 Things You Need To Know About A Highly Sexual Single Woman — 35
9.  6 Reasons To Sleep With Whomever You Want Without Regret — 41
10. 5 Surprising Ways A Woman Decides Whether Or Not They Want To Sleep With You — 45
11. 7 Real Life Reasons You Can't Get It Up — 49
12. 8 Things She Never Wants To Hear You Say — 53
13. 5 Reasons Summer Is The Best Time To Get Into A Relationship — 57
14. How To Avoid A Bad First Date — 61
15. How To (Respectfully) Date Multiple Men At Once — 67
16. What You're Really Saying To The Chick(s) You Let Crash At Your Place — 71
17. How To Tell If You're Getting Played By A Woman With Serious Game — 75
18. 5 Telltale Signs That You're More Into Them Than They're Into You — 81
19. 7 Responses To "What Are We?" That Let You Know Exactly WTF Is Up — 85

| | | |
|---|---|---|
| 20. | How Long Should I Wait For Someone To "Be Ready" To Commit? | 89 |
| 21. | The Secret To Every Woman's Heart | 91 |
| 22. | What It's Like To Date A Woman On Her Shit | 95 |
| 23. | Do It For The Gram: 3 Reasons Why Your Girlfriend Wants You To Show Her Off | 99 |
| 24. | How Being A Mom Made Me More Desirable To Men | 103 |
| 25. | 15 Signs Your Relationship Is On The Right Track | 109 |
| 26. | 5 Ways To Show Her You Care (That Won't Cost You Anything) | 115 |
| 27. | 5 Ways To Show Him You Care (That Won't Cost You Anything) | 117 |
| 28. | 5 Things You Seriously Do NOT Need To Talk About In Your Relationship | 119 |
| 29. | These Things Are Never Worth Fighting About In Your Relationship | 123 |
| 30. | 5 Foolproof Ways To Improve Your Relationship | 127 |
| 31. | 7 Things You'll Learn When Shacking Up | 131 |
| 32. | What He Means When He Says 'I Need Space' (And How To Deal With It) | 137 |
| 33. | 7 Signs You're In Relationship Limbo | 141 |
| 34. | How To Apologize When You (Really) Fucked Up | 145 |
| 35. | 5 Obvious Signs You're With The Wrong Person | 151 |
| 36. | 10 Reasons To Be Thankful For A Broken Heart | 155 |
| 37. | 4 Things You Get Better At Every Time You Get Cheated On | 161 |
| 38. | 10 Signs You're Not Over Your Ex (No Matter How Much You Want To Be) | 165 |
| 39. | 10 Mature Reasons To Be Friends With Your Ex | 169 |
| 40. | 5 Things You Need To Remember When You're Feeling Really Fucking Lonely | 173 |
| **About the Author** | | 177 |

# 1

# Why You Should Take Relationship Advice From Me

As if the world needs another book on how to do relationships right, right?

I agree with you, but this one will be different. The further into this book you read, the more you'll notice just how different it is. I'm not here to give you the secret formula for a perfect relationship. Hell, I've never been in a relationship longer than 10 months—but for good reason. I want the real thing and I will not settle for anything less! Here are a few reasons why you should take relationship advice from me. Let's get into it!

## I still believe in true love.

I know it's real. I don't think everyone will get the privilege of experiencing it, but it's definitely real. If you're going to take relationship advice from someone, it should be from someone who still looks at true love as a real possibility, not someone who is still hurting from or bitter about past relationships.

## I'm a hopeless romantic.

Naturally, I am a hopeless romantic. How else would I still believe in true love? Although I've never had anyone do even a third of what I can suggest as far as romancing someone goes, it's my thing…and I don't mean flowers on the first date romantic. I'm next level—we're talking watching the sunset by way of an evening picnic-style dinner on the beach here, people. I'm legit.

## I'm a self-proclaimed sexpert.

I love sex. I love everything I've learned about it so far. I've done my fair share of experiencing just about everything there is to know about sex, orgasms, and why you should have a life filled with great sex. As a very "share the wealth" type of person, why wouldn't I give great advice on how to have the kind of sex that would make any relationship full of life?

## I don't mind finding out I'm wrong.

At the end of the day, I don't know everything and I am completely okay with that. I don't mind finding out that The One wasn't really the one. I don't mind entering relationships that I see potential in because you lose 100% of the shots you don't take. This is why I've never been in a relationship beyond 10 months. I don't allow my time to be wasted and I wouldn't waste anyone else's time.

So grab a glass of wine or a cup of coffee and keep reading. You won't regret it.

# 2

# How To Slide In The Direct Messages

Trying to talk to someone online doesn't seem that hard, right? Not if you're the really charismatic online kind of person, but let's be real here...not all of you are. Social media has become one of the top ways that society stays connected with the people and things going on around them. With that being said, I am not against people who make friends online. I know a few couples who started dating after they met online, in fact. However, this is not an article about online dating, this is an article about the first step–properly starting conversation online. It's easy to speak to anyone online if it's done publicly like commenting on a status or picture, but that's not really the same as starting a one-on-one conversation. It's after you try to slide into the DMs that you find yourself having some difficulty soliciting a response (especially with the cattiness of some people these days). What's sliding into the DMs, you ask? For those of you who are unaware of the lingo, DMs are direct private messages to an individual on a social media site like Facebook or Twitter. You might be thinking to yourself, "I don't need help talking to people online...the stuff I say is as smooth as cream cheese on a bagel." Okay...maybe you're not saying that particularly, but you get my drift. You feel like you don't need help in this department, but I can assure you that the next tips I give you are ones you should definitely hold onto when attempting to start a conversation online. Let's get into it!

## Say the right kind of "Hello."

All too often do I have to correct the way a man 'slides into my DMs' just based off of how he addresses me. Although, "What's up, beautiful?" may sound like a winning opening line to you…it is a MAJOR turnoff for most women. A simple "Hi, how are you?" will do in most cases. I think the other thing to take into consideration when choosing the right greeting is whether or not you know the person you're messaging. If you don't know them, always go with a normal greeting. Compliments are nice, but coming from a stranger it can be a little weird if done incorrectly. In all honesty, it takes a smooth delivery to offer a compliment in a way that engages a someone without them feeling creeped out by you being a complete stranger.

## Do a little research.

Yes, I think it's important to do a little 'research' on the person you're about to message. Especially if you're introducing yourself online to someone you do not know personally. No, I'm not telling you to go 52 weeks into their Instagram or to go and dig up old tagged photos on Facebook, but at least read their bio and a few of their recent status updates, so that you can get a feel for what to say to them and how to say it. This is also where it is appropriate to find something to compliment them on. With women, most of us have the things we are proud of in our bio and on statuses, so this is another way to open a conversation.

**\*\*EXCLUSIVE TIP OF THE YEAR:** If they are in a relationship and you don't have any other reason besides a 'personal' one to message them–I have no idea why I have to say this, but I do–leave them alone. No, they're probably not interested in being your "friend." If you're capable of having a respectful conversation with an actual point or maybe you're messaging them about business, then that's a different story, but always respect the relationship.\*\*

## Have fruitful conversation to offer.

Piggybacking off the previous point, when you do a little research it should give you good insight on appropriate conversation starters. One way to definitely get me conversing with you online is to share your opinion on a recent status or article that I have written because I love to hear people's thoughts on those things. If you look into their profile just a little bit or you're familiar with the things that strike their interest as a result of following them, it shouldn't be hard to have fruitful conversation. Have something to offer when you slide into their inbox. Don't be inappropriate. Don't be rude or insulting. Don't just say 'hey' and then expect them to just dive into a conversation with you when you messaged them first.

## Have a point.

Hopefully there is some type of point behind you're messaging them. I have plenty of online friends that I have made. I don't meet many of them, especially if there are no mutual friends or we don't live in the same area and happen to run into each other out somewhere. But, I do make connections with plenty of amazing people online. When you reach out to them and get the conversation started, have a point behind doing it even if it's you just wanting to discuss your opinion about their most recent post. Otherwise, it can come off a bit creepy that you "just wanted to say hello" to someone you don't know at all.

## Don't ask them for their number, offer yours.

After a few successful online conversations with them, if the two of you decide to continue speaking to one another, do not ask for their number. You are the one that initiated the conversation, so you need to be the one to follow it all the way through. Kindly let them know that you enjoyed the conversations you two have had and that if they would like to, they can connect with you via phone call or text. That is much more appropriate than asking for their number and it gives them the refreshing option of contacting you at their convenience, instead of having to feel vulnerable about your ability to contact them at your freewill.

Don't underestimate the power of conversation, even if it happens to start online! Most people love to be flattered by intellect. Start a valuable conversation and watch how beautifully things escalate between the two of you.

# 3

# How To Talk To Someone You're Interested In On The Phone

I'll be honest in saying a lot of people claim to not like talking on the phone anymore. Don't trust that this kind of person is the kind of person you want to pursue a relationship with. If they can't talk to you on the phone, how will they converse with you face to face? That's just a disclaimer. Anyway, we've talked about how to start a conversation online. Now, that you've got their number, let's discuss what that conversation should be like. Here's how to talk to someone you're interested in on the phone. Let's get into it!

## Be available.

First things first, don't call if you don't have time to talk. There is nothing more annoying than someone calling you to tell you that they'll call you back. Yes, we understand that some things are sporadic and that's understandable. For the most part though, make sure you're free and available to hold at least a 15-30 minute uninterrupted conversation with the person you're talking to. Show them that they are worth your time and undivided attention.

## Ask questions that spark conversation.

When you two begin to engage in conversation, make it easy for yourself. Don't ask questions that are conversation killers unless you're fully prepared to spark a conversation from their answer (which is pretty hard to do for most). The conversation killers are the common:

*How are you?*—Another way to ask this question is, "You sound like you're in a good mood. What's going on?" That will encourage them to 1. Acknowledge that they are indeed in a good mood and 2. Share with you what caused their good mood.

*What are you up to?*—If you're a good conversationalist, you can start conversation from this based on their answer, still I don't suggest it. Instead of asking what they are doing first, you could tell then what you're doing and then ask what they've done or will do with their day. You choosing to elaborate on the happenings of your day will encourage them to do the same instead of just responding by saying "I'm not doing anything."

*How was your day?*—I know that you think this is a great conversation starter, but it's not. It's a nice thing to ask, but most people will simply reply with "It was good/bad." Instead, ask them what the highlight of their day was. They'll have to 1. Think about what they did today and choose their best moment and 2. Elaborate on why that was the highlight of their day. The fact that you asked then what the best part of their day was will definitely make them smile. Trust me.

For a deeper conversation, try to ask questions that will cause them to answer with a few sentences or more. Spark deeper conversation by asking questions like:

*What are your aspirations?*
*Where is your ideal place to live?*
*What is your idea of the perfect date?*

## Listen and respond.

Women love to talk, but so do men. If you say the right things, you'll learn that people can pretty much have a conversation with themselves. Intrigue them enough and they could literally carry the conversation alone, only leaving space for you to harmlessly interject every now and then. If you are a conversationalist, you'll know how to move in and out of the conversation, but if you're not really one to talk a lot just ask the right stuff… They'll handle the rest. The more important part is to make sure you're listening. If you don't listen, you can't respond—which will kill the conversation altogether. Offer feedback, tell your answer to whatever you're asking them—be engaged.

## Let the conversation flow.

If you're finding that you're having trouble keeping the conversation flowing and you know that you're asking the right types of questions and you're open to conversation, that's probably a sign that you're on the phone with the wrong person. Conversation is natural; it flows. If you're doing too much work to keep it alive, do yourself the favor of thanking them for their time, but I'd start looking to call someone else. It's okay to realize that this particular person is not the person for you. In terms of dating, you probably won't have a very successful relationship with someone you can't have good conversation with.

## Be genuine.

This is important. Don't say things you think they want to hear. Be genuine. This will help things flow. It will also relax you and allow you to listen and respond better. If you're focused on what you should say to impress them, then you won't be able to really listen to anything that they're saying. When you let your guard down and remain genuine in your conversation, not only will you be able to listen and respond to what they're saying with ease, but they'll probably love everything you're saying as well.

## Leave them thinking.

There is such a thing as having too long of a conversation. I know you don't think so, but seriously. The first conversation is usually much longer than the ones to come because both of you are trying to get to know each other, but leave some for later. Don't spill out all your guts the first go-around. You want to leave them thinking about the next conversation you two will have. End the conversation letting them know that you enjoyed speaking to them, but you've got to go for now. Now they're probably thinking about things they want to ask you next time so that they can listen and respond. They're also probably wondering if you'll remember anything they've said from this conversation. They're probably even thinking about how sexy your voice is. No matter what thoughts they're having, they're thinking about you. This is a great thing and will definitely guarantee another phone call in the future.

You've got their attention, so don't waste it. Although we appreciate the morning text, offer them a little bit more as well. You're well on your way to being quite the conversationalist. So, go ahead and give them a call on your lunch break. You got this. I know they can't wait to hear from you.

# 4

# 4 Topics (Pretty Much) Anybody Loves To Talk About

I've noticed recently that we talk a lot about the importance of conversation and communication, but I've never really specified what sorts of things people like to talk about. So, here are four topics (pretty much) anybody loves to talk about. Let's get into it!

## 1. Their latest project or endeavor.

Naturally, people enjoy talking about themselves. Most people love being able to share their latest ideas with a listening ear. The big event she's been planning for weeks now, or the next city he'll be traveling to with you. Nothing makes them happier than knowing you're interested in what they're working on or where they're going in life. It means a lot to them and therefore, they want it to mean a lot to you. The next time you're sitting down to dinner with them, instead of asking an open-ended question about what they did today, be specific and ask them what the latest project they've been developing is about or what big plans they have for their new business, event, or even a holiday.

## 2. Favorites.

It doesn't only have to be their favorite things. People like these types of conversation appetizers, as I'll call them, because they'll get the conversation started. You'll start off asking things like their favorite color, but eventually you'll roll up on a favorite that you both have in common and the conversation is sure to flow from there. Whether you get into talk about a certain time period you both miss because you have the same favorite song or you find out that you both love the same football team…I'm sure the conversation will have plenty of meaty goodness from there on out as you get to know each other.

## 3. Your future plans.

We absolutely want to know what your plans for your future are. We want to know what kind of car you're expecting to drive in five years. We want to know whether or not you have a desire to get married and start a family or if you'd rather live in a loft in Downtown L.A. by yourself. These types of things are really important and naturally people will get into these details without being primed first. So, next time instead of waiting on them to ask you first or to bring it up on their own, just jump right in and wow them with where you're headed in life!

## 4. Sex.

This one is kind of tricky, but still it would be a lie if I said this was not one of the things people enjoy talking about. We want the conversation to be tasteful and there is definitely a right time and place, but when the time is right and the conversation is sexy, not provocative... People love it. Trust me. Now, again the conversation MUST be tasteful, which means instead of saying "Damn girl, I want you to sit on my face," we'd much rather hear, "I enjoy pleasuring a woman with my tongue" instead. We'll comprehend the message the same way, but it won't piss us off and make us think you're in it to please yourself and not us. That's the key. People want to hear what you'd like to do to them for the sake of their pleasure, not yours. What can I say? People want to be put first!

# 5

# 3 Reasons To Go For The One Who Is Not Your Type

We don't like to admit it much, but I believe we all have certain qualities we look for in a potential mate. There's nothing wrong with that. Sure, I say that "I don't have a type..." just like the rest of us, but really what I mean when I say that is that I wouldn't be closed minded about getting to know anybody. To be honest, I fall in love with people every day. I look at character far more than I look at anything else in a person. That doesn't mean that I don't prefer darker men to lighter men or that I'm not crazy about a man with a bald head and a beard. Nevertheless, those things are not deciding factors in my choosing to get to know someone better. I find that most times, when I do decide to go after someone that I want, they hardly ever fit that typical person I see in my mind anyway. I end up building genuine relationships with the person who actually isn't much like the person I see in my head a lot. I won't deny that I feel pretty shallow at first, but we'll get to that. Here are three good reasons to go for the one who's not your type. Let's get into it!

# 1. It takes you out of your comfort zone.

Just like anything else worth having, it's highly unlikely that you will find the right person for you inside of your comfort zone. Usually when I go after someone who I usually wouldn't go for, it causes me to have to approach the entire situation completely different than I'm used to. I have to think of fresh ways to present myself and I have to open myself up to receive that person in whatever ways they may present themselves to me. It's quite refreshing to be honest. It's the authentic 'getting to know' you moment. You have to really get to learn about that person and they have to do the same for you. It's likely that you two will still find things you have in common, but you'll have differences, too, which is always fun and interesting.

# 2. You'll find better qualities to value in them.

When you go for someone who isn't necessarily your type, you won't be distracted by the qualities you usually look for in someone. That will allow you to open your eyes to many of the qualities you overlook because of what you're used to. You will be able to see and appreciate the finer qualities of that person, which again makes for a great 'getting to know you' stage. As you learn more about that person you will learn to value the very things that set them apart from the kind of person you usually go for.

# 3. It's a new experience.

If nothing else in life, we should always want to experience something fresh and new. It's no different with finding new friends and pursuing new relationships. It's important to want to experience new things with someone. It's almost inevitable that if you pursue someone who you usually wouldn't, the two of you will enjoy a good bit of new experiences together. This, for me, is the most exhilarating part of going after the guy I usually wouldn't approach. It's what keeps me coming back.

I hope that this encourages you to go out and look for something a little different than you usually do. I also hope this gives you just a little bit more hope that love is out there for all of us. It may not look, feel, or be the way we imagine it, but it's for the better.

# <u>6</u>

# 5 Reasons To Date Your Friend

I used to think I was doing myself a favor by instantly friend-zoning the men I met. I make new friends like strippers make money—frequently, at a high volume, and with very little effort. With that, I found life a lot less complicated when I only established platonic friendships. As I grew older though, all of that changed for me. I realized that the reason I felt that there were no good men left to date is because I was friends with all my candidates! So, what was a girl to do? I didn't leave myself any other option, and I'm glad that I didn't. Here are five good reasons to date one of your friends. Let's get into it!

## 1. You already know their character flaws.

No, they are not perfect. In fact, they're far from it. Still, there are a bunch of qualities in them that you really care for. Since you two have been friends, you're already sure of what their character flaws are (and they know yours, too). This makes things like getting cheated on and other relationship red flags easy to see if they ever become present. Depending on the level of maturity and depth of the friendship, it also eliminates the risk of pesky arguments. For example, if you know they aren't that good of a listener, you won't be mad when you two are dating and they don't listen to you as attentively as you want them to right then.

## 2. Deep down, you always wanted to date them anyway.

Face it. We don't really make friends without thinking to ourselves (even if it's just for a second), could I date them? Most of the greatest parts of your life will be a result of taking risks—that goes for relationships, too.

## 3. You can skip the "Getting to Know You" stage.

Okay, maybe not skip it altogether, but you'll experience it differently. You two won't be going through those fifty million awkward questions and instead will be spending time getting to know the sappy, sweet side of your friend turned lover. You'll be getting to know the freaky side of your friend turned lover. You'll finally learn the answers to all the things you used to wonder about your friend turned lover. It's exhilarating, really.

## 4. You can develop a deep, intimate relationship.

As a result of getting to know your friend on a deeper level, you two will naturally develop an intimate relationship with one another. You'll connect on a level that neither of you imagined beforehand. You'll be connected to a point where you know exactly what makes them happy, sad, mad—you name it. If you thought that your friendship was fruitful, just watch where being connected on this level takes the two of you as you embark on a romantic relationship.

## 5. It's so crazy that it just might work.

At the end of the day, you may learn that your friend was the one you were looking for all along. The thing about this, though? You won't know until you try!

If you've been feeling in your gut that you should tell your friend how you really feel about them, let this be the nudge you needed. Go get 'em!

# 7

# 15 Of The Sexiest Things Any Man Can Do

Who says you have to be Ryan Gosling or Idris Elba to be sexy?

I believe any man can be sexy. Contrary to popular belief, looks really don't hold a lot of weight in the sexy category. Furthermore, the simplicity of the sexiest things a man can do will blow your mind. You ready? Let's get into it.

## 1. Teach me something.

An intelligent man is a gift from the good Lord himself. Please notice I didn't say educated. I'm a firm believer that 'street smarts' outweigh 'book smarts' any day. Sorry/not sorry. Just because you went to college does not mean you're smart. God bless the man with his degree, but I'm here for you men who are able to operate by way of good home training and other gifts and talents as well. The man who is able to teach me something will forever be a treasure in my eyes.

## 2. Have good taste in music.

Women find your taste in music extremely sexy, especially when it's the kind of music she likes. If she's not familiar with the music you listen to she'll find it even sexier if you can make your style of music appealing to her. You definitely get extra points if you can sing or play an instrument. We melt!

## 3. Own and work the room.

It goes without saying that a confident man is unearthly sexy to women. What is even sexier than you being a confident man is when we see that confident man in action. If you've never done so before, invite a woman to join you at an office party or really any type of event that will showcase your ability to own and work a room. She'll follow you the entire time and become astounded at how sexy it is to watch you handle yourself in this environment.

## 4. Two words: basketball shorts.

Yep. You know what I'm talking about. If you don't like basketball shorts, sweatpants, or pajama bottoms have the same effect. We're crazy about it!

## 5. Look good in a suit.

Extra points if you wear a bow tie. We love to see you dressed down, but we can hardly control ourselves when you're able to dress up and do it nicely. Just another little tip, the socks matter. I'm a fool for a man who wears those colorful, fun dress socks with a tailored suit and tie.

## 6. Smell good.

You knew that though. If you haven't figured this one out yet, take the time to find a signature cologne you can wear all the time. There are certain fragrances that instantly remind me of the man I know who wears that particular fragrance. No matter where I smell it, he always comes rushing back to my mind. You want to have this effect on women—trust me. Another tip, it makes hugs and sex that much better...just saying.

## 7. Read.

A man who reads can teach me something new. A man who reads takes advantage of his free time. A man who reads is intelligent. A man who reads is ambitious. A man who reads values the opinion of others. A man who reads wants to know more than what people are willing to tell him. A man who reads is patient. A man who reads is SEXY.

## 8. Maintain relationships of all kinds (religious, business, friends, and family).

Take heed to the different types of relationships I point out here. Yes, they all matter—at least to me. A man who can maintain these relationships is usually genuine, honest, and trustworthy. He values each of these types of relationships and is an asset within the relationship as well. Does that make sense? A relationship is a two-way street. A healthy relationship of any kind takes commitment. If you're able to maintain personal relationships of these types then you obviously understand what it takes to build and maintain a long-lasting romantic relationship.

## 9. Be ambitious.

God knows I think a man with ambition is just about as sexy as it gets. An ambitious man is strong and passionate in everything that he does. This kind of man wins not because he has achieved something (although that is amazing, too), but because he has a hunger to want to achieve things. This kind of man is patient with the process of achievement. This kind of man likes to be encouraged and understands the importance of being encouraged and supported.

## 10. Be a little bit of a bad boy.

You know why good guys finish last? Because as stupid as it sounds, women love a man who lives on the edge—just a little. We want a man who has the ability to put his foot down without stepping on us. We want a man to be able to (respectfully) "put us in our place." We want a man who can make a sarcastic comment without being known as the asshole or the douchebag—there's a fine line here, so be careful. A little edginess goes a long way though—don't push it.

## 11. Have a healthy sense of humor.

Who doesn't love a man who can make you laugh? A man

with a healthy sense of humor is extremely sexy. We want you to be able to be silly with us. We want you to laugh at our joke that really isn't all that funny. We want you to be able to make us laugh 'the laugh' that we hate to do in public.

## 12. Expose your forearms.

I'm serious. A man in a collared shirt with the top few buttons undone and the sleeves rolled up to just below the elbow is bound to make most women hot in the pants. It's safe to say that it's much like the effect cleavage has on you men. It's masculine and sexy. To me, it even gives off a 'free' sort of vibe. Rolling your sleeves up kind of says, "I'm here and I'm ready to relax and have a good time." Bonus points if you have tattoos!

## 13. Keep your body hair under control.

Yes, we want you to keep all of your body hair under control. You don't have to shave everything, but we want you to keep things trimmed. I'm not a fan of taco meat, so I'd prefer that to be shaved, but not all women are like that. I don't have a problem with armpit hair, but it shouldn't be so long that you can braid it. I also don't have a problem with pubic hair, but it should always be well-groomed. You don't want us harboring a small forest down there and we don't want that from you either. Let's be fair.

## 14. Grow a beard.

You still need to keep it neat, but a full beard is so sexy. My goodness, the thoughts that come to my mind when I see a man with a nice beard. I have no idea what it is about it, fellas. Nevertheless, it is always a win for most of us women. We love a manly man with a nice beard—and if you have nice lips you may as well grab a mop because I'm sure we've left a puddle on the floor. Okay, just some light humor there, but seriously. If you have the ability to grow a nice beard…try it some time.

## 15. Hold a conversation.

Women love to talk. A man who can create, engage, and end a conversation appropriately is very sexy! I've seen several articles that highlight the sexiness of a man who can hold a conversation, but you know what really turns me on about a man I can engage in conversation with? His ability to end the conversation in a manner that leaves the conversation on my mind and that leaves me wanting more! That's a sure-fire way to guarantee that you'll hear from me again.

There you have it, Gents—the sexiest things any man can do. You'll notice that most of these things are practically effortless and none of them involve sex, but we'll tackle that next time. In the meantime between time, give these a shot.

# 8

# 15 Things You Need To Know About A Highly Sexual Single Woman

I am now, as I always have been, very comfortable in my sexuality. Unfortunately, there are so many stereotypes, double standards, and wrongful judgments that come with being a highly sexual woman, but I'm going to make some of those things clear right now. Here are 15 things you need to know about the life of a highly sexual single woman. Let's get into it!

## 1. Sex can be emotional, but it doesn't have to be.

This is arguably the most misunderstood fact about being a highly sexual woman. Sex can and most times is completely physical for the woman indulging. This isn't only for women who are highly sexual beings. Yes fellas, it was just sex. It's stress relieving and therapeutic. Thanks for your time. Buh-bye now.

## 2. Masturbation is a way of life.

No shame in the masturbation game. At this point, you don't

even need the porn. A candlelit bubble bath and wine is all I need to get this party started.

## 3. Men are both intrigued and intimidated by you.

This is arguably the most frustrating fact about being a highly sexual woman. Your sexuality is astounding to them (especially if they've heard anything [true or false] about you), but your sexual freedom intimidates their masculinity as well. Don't let them tell you different. It's true. It takes a very solid man to deal with our kind.

## 4. You're either a sex god or a whore in the eyes of others.

Simple as that. You can't just be a confident woman who is comfortable with her sexuality—oh no. For most, you're either a sex legend or a walking with a scarlet letter. The end.

## 5. All of your friends come to you for sexual How Tos and advice.

I actually enjoy this part of being a highly sexual woman and other women like me are fond of it, too. Because we're comfortable in our sexual behaviors, it's nice to shed a little light on why and how we are this way. For me personally, I like to educate my friends and really anyone else who asks me questions so that they can find their sexuality as exhilarating and enjoyable as I do.

## 6. Sometimes she'll quit after one hit.

The only thing worse than no sex at all is BAD sex. Period. You can bet your bottom dollar that you only get one shot to 'wow' a highly sexual woman one time. Should you disappoint, she will NOT be back for seconds. I promise.

## 7. "I fuck who I want, and fuck who I don't."

That's the bottom line. It's never as many people as others would think, but either way we don't look at it as numbers. A highly sexual woman has the leisure of picking her partners just as carefully as she chooses her selfies. When you engage in a highly sexual woman it's because she chose you too. Believe that!

## 8. You get very few bad reviews.

A bad report doesn't happen often, if at all. It's a moment of pride for us to share our sexual drive and passion with those that we choose to experience it.

## 9. There is a difference between sex and love.

Again, this is another one of those myths that will really frustrate a highly sexual woman because so many people feel that we aren't able to connect or disconnect love and sex. Just because I am a highly sexual woman does not by any means mean that I cannot be faithfully committed to one partner.

## 10. A healthy, lasting relationship is a very possible thing.

For those of you who do identify yourselves as a highly sexual woman…do not for any reason let the judgment of others force you to believe that the previously mentioned is not true and obtainable.

## 11. Nothing hurts like "Not now, babe."

At this point in the life of a highly sexual woman, her desire for her partner burns passionately…pretty much all the time. Now, it's no mystery that her urge to make love will be stronger than her partners, but that doesn't make the rejection for fun time hurt any less.

## 12. Multiple times a day is not me being spoiled, it's exercise!

Again, when a highly sexual woman finds a man that can handle her and wants to be with her and only her, that passion for him is I N T E N S E to say the least. That means that yes, 10 times out of 10—she's hot in the pants for her man and if he lets her get it, she's gonna go for it every time.

## 13. You constantly want to try new things.

A lot of love-making means you have to keep things innovative and fresh to make sure that you two wear each other out (winky face), but don't get tired of one another. A highly sexual woman understands the importance of going all out to keep her man happy and to keep the relationship on the up-and-up. There's always new tricks to learn.

## 14. You have to be with a highly sexual man.

This I am willing to debate, but from my own personal experience…relationships have been healthiest for me when I was committed to someone with as strong a sexuality as my own. What do you think?

## 15. Sex with you is an experience.

I'm willing to bet that any man who is in a relationship with a highly sexual woman has little to no complaints about the intimacy the two of them share. The passionate, wild, sensual connection you share with someone you're growing with is incomparable at least while it lasts.

# 9

# 6 Reasons To Sleep With Whomever You Want Without Regret

You wouldn't even be reading this right now if it weren't for the sex your parents had years ago! So why do we deny ourselves the opportunity to participate in such a beautiful experience? It's more than likely because you're fearful of what someone might think of you. Sleeping with whoever you want doesn't mean you have to sleep around. Slow and steady wins the race and I'd suggest one guy at a time, but you don't have to try and stick to having sex with only three people in your lifetime. I mean, let's face it—most of us passed that limit a long time ago. Whether you're afraid of what people would think of you or if you're looking for some clarification on why it's okay to do it, here are six reasons to sleep with who you want without regret. Let's get into it!

## 1. Sex is beautiful.

Like I said, mistake or not, you wouldn't have the breath of life if it weren't for your parents having some (hopefully mind-blowing) sex. Sex is a beautiful experience that should be shared with someone special; it doesn't mean you have to give them your whole life because you chose them to be that special person. Sure, it's a plus if the two of you fall in love and decide to sleep with each other for the rest of your lives, but how often does that happen these days?

## 2. Sex does not devalue your human worth.

Contrary to popular belief, your human worth does not decrease with the number of times you've had sex. You're not a car and you don't have mileage. Hopefully, out of self-respect, you won't overdo it. Partaking in sexual activity is special, as I've said already. When you participate, you should remember that at all times. Don't have sex with just anybody; don't have sex unless you want to; and have passionate, mind-blowing sex every single time. You won't steer yourself wrong or have any regrets if you keep those three things in mind.

## 3. Nobody has to know.

No if, ands, or buts about it. The only people who need to know about the sexual encounters you've had are inside your head—or am I the only one who has voices in their head? This is another reason why it's so important to make sure you're choosing the right kind of people to share a sexual experience with. Don't sleep with someone who can't keep it to themselves. Your sex life is your business, period.

## 4. There are major health benefits to having sex.

Just Google it if you don't believe me. Why should you deny

yourself a healthier lifestyle because you're afraid of what someone might think of you?

## 5. If your limit is three to five, you're bound to max out before you find "the one."

Finding love is hard as fuck. If you've set a limit for yourself, you'll probably do one of two things – pass it or settle. Instead of worrying about a limit, just engage. Don't feel bad about it and take a chance at finding love in a way that's a lot more fun!

## 6. Sexual contact is a natural desire—it's okay!

We all get horny. We all think about sex. It's natural and more importantly, it's nothing to be ashamed about! As long as you're choosing partners that care about their health and you're maintaining yours, as well, engage in a healthy sex life. You don't have to regret sleeping with different people. Again, you should not sleep with multiple people at once, but you can sleep with more than three people in your lifetime.

Get out there and live!

# 10

# 5 Surprising Ways A Woman Decides Whether Or Not They Want To Sleep With You

Do you think men think about sex more than women do? Maybe, but I'll tell you what, a lot more women think about sex than you might be aware of. Although we don't just come out and say it like some guys do, there are certain things we associate with your skills in bed from the very minute we meet you. I'm sure you've heard the saying, "first impressions are lasting" and that couldn't be more true! I won't lie, most of the things I'm about to point out are influenced by my wild sense of imagination, but still they are some things to keep in mind. Here are five ways a woman decides whether or not they want to sleep with you. Let's get into it!

## 1. Your appearance.

Remember when all women obsessed over the thought of Christian Grey from *50 Shades*? One of the things that made him such a fantasy was the way he kept his appearance up. If you haven't realized what your style of dress (or the lack thereof) does for a woman then start paying closer attention.

We are instantly intrigued by a well-dressed man, but when your overall appearance is complete and done just right, you've got our full attention. Now, what does it mean for your appearance to be just right? It means you're dressed properly, groomed properly (yes, including your nails), good-smelling, facial hair well kept—good hygiene. Ultimately, women want a man that can walk into a room and grab more than just her attention…we perceive it very sexy and very manly. If you look the part, we wouldn't hesitate to daydream about how well you handle yourself in bed.

## 2. Your grip.

I'm not talking about how you dap your friends up when you see them. For a woman, whether it's from a hug or a hand-shake, this association is influenced by the desire women have for a manly man as well. We like to think of your grip as the grasp you'll take of our body if the time for a sexual encounter ever became real. Eye contact. In control. Firm, but not harsh. Solid, but not hard. Protective, all while being as gentle as we need you to be. YES. YES. YES. This puts a good deal of thoughts in our mind about how you will handle us in the bedroom.

## 3. Your taste in music.

I may very well be alone in this association, but I'm convinced that a man who listens to classics—like real classics—knows exactly how to handle a woman in bed. I just can't force myself to believe that someone who doesn't have a "broad" taste in music knows how to properly treat a woman in the bedroom. I just can't. I need you to be able to throw on tunes that you know will put me in the mood, not music that makes me want to slap the person next to me. Correct me if I'm wrong, but many women fantasize about making love while soft and sexy love songs play in the background.

## 4. Your dance skills.

The only thing I love more than dancing alone is dancing with a man who can keep up! I mean seriously, I can't get over how sexy a man who can hang with me on the dance floor is. I get that all men don't like to dance, so if you don't dance because you can't dance…don't feel bad. However, if you're a man who likes to dance, take a woman out dancing and tell me all about what I know will be a fantastic night for the two of you. I'm not talking about knowing the latest YouTube dance moves either; I'm talking about really stepping. Whether slow and steady or a little more upbeat, a confident, dancing man is surely a sight to see and the perfect recipe for a wild day-dream. I absolutely associate how smooth you can be on the dance floor with how well you dance in bed.

## 5. Your conversation.

Again, this association is heavily influenced by the desire women have for a manly man. Intelligence is extremely sexy. When you're able to be mature enough to develop chemistry and carry a real conversation with a woman, I don't doubt that you can't create that same chemistry with a woman in the bedroom. Listening and responding is all it takes to keep a woman's attention in conversation. On the other hand, if you're all over the place and unfocused during conversation, I presume you'd be the same way in bed.

Like I said, most of these things are influenced by my wild sense of imagination, but still they are some things to keep in mind the next time you meet a lady you find yourself interested in.

# 11

# 7 Real Life Reasons You Can't Get It Up

Let me introduce you to the absolute greatest "no-no" in the doss and don'tss of sex—not being able to get it up. I shared with you what it's like being a highly sexual woman and I'm telling you, nothing is more offensive than you going limp during sex or not even being able to get it up in the first place. If you're mind is preoccupied, it's okay to say "Baby, not tonight." There's nothing worse than being in the mood and your soldier decides he's not fighting any battles tonight. You may not have tried to do so intentionally and I get that, but that doesn't make it any less offensive! Here are 7 real life reasons you can't get it up. Let's get into it!

## 1. You're stressed out.

Although sex is a wonderful stress reliever, you might be so stressed out that you lack the physical ability to have an erection. Determine what the source of the stress is so that you can handle it head-on and you'll find that once you deal with the stress, it won't be so hard to get it up.

## 2. You're irritated.

Sometimes you're just not in the mood; don't force it.

## 3. Smoking.

Smoking didn't used to bother me, but it really is a dirty habit. It also puts so much of your health at risk. Not only is it a turn-off that you can't get it up, but realizing that your body is functioning like it's twice your actual age on account of cigarettes is really unattractive and a major turn-off as well.

## 4. You're out of energy.

We want you to be healthy. We don't want to go all night every night, but when the time is right, we need your stamina to be in excellent conditions. If you're out of energy, you'll learn that you might not have trouble getting it up, but keeping it up and keeping up with her in bed is sure to be a hassle for you.

## 5. You're worried you won't perform well.

It's natural for us to doubt ourselves when trying something for the first time. If you find that you're having a little performance anxiety, take a deep breath and let it go! Most women won't tell you if you're bad at it anyway. Go ahead and get you some!

## 6. Alcohol and drugs.

As much as people think drunk and high sex is so riveting, it can also have a negative effect on your functionality. In other words, no matter how much you're turned on, getting a hard on might not be as easy as it seems. Don't be so under any influence that you no longer have control over your bodily functions.

## 7. You're just not that into her.

We never want to admit it, but sometimes this is exactly the reason. You could love everything about her, but we'd be in major denial if we acted as if sexual satisfaction wasn't a factor in a healthy relationship. The best thing to do in this situation would be to be honest with her. Make sure she understands the things you do like about her and maybe even let her know how she could improve—but be careful with this. If she's willing to try and improve—great; if not, be understanding and move on.

# 12

# 8 Things She Never Wants To Hear You Say

Have you ever said something that (you thought) was completely harmless and all of a sudden your girlfriend or girl friend got really pissed off out of nowhere? *Trigger sayings.* At least that's what I call them. My advice to you is to stay as far away from them as you possibly can to avoid this situation from happening anymore. Here are eight things she never wants to hear you say. Let's get into it!

## 1. "I don't know."

No matter what the question is, the last answer she want to hear from you is that you don't know because to her, it means you didn't even think about the question and therefore, you don't care. When she makes the effort to change her hairstyle or makes other efforts to "be great" for you, DO NOT say that you don't know if you like it or not. She needs a solid answer from you about these things. She really cares about your opinion—most times.

## 2. "I don't care."

The only thing worse than telling her that you don't know is telling her out loud that you don't care. It's extremely frustrating because she wouldn't have asked you the question if she didn't want you to care. This answer can make you look like a major asshole, especially depending on what the question was to begin with.

## 3. "What's up with your friend?"

Um, what? Don't ever ask a woman to hook you up with her friends. If you want to talk to her, then go over there and do just that. Asking a woman to "put in a good word for you" is in the same boat. Call it what you want, but no woman wants to hear you say that. If she wanted you and her friend to take a shot at anything she would have introduced you two without you having to ask. Just FYI.

## 4. "Why do you have on all that makeup?"

She has it on because it makes her look and feel good. No, she doesn't need it, but she likes it. Women understand that you men "love" us in our natural state, but just think of it as an enhancer. We don't wear it because we feel ugly without it, we just KNOW we look amazing with it!

## 5. "Is that what you're wearing?"

First of all, it probably took her about an hour or two to get extra sexy for wherever it is you two are going, and as she comes out of the room feeling like a million dollars, you steal her glorious feeling by asking if that is what she is choosing to wear. Now, it's totally fine to not like what she is wearing, but don't question it. Just let her know how you feel about it—especially if you love what she has on. Tell her how sexy she looks. A lady needs to hear these things.

## 6. Almost anything you can say about another woman that you should have said to her first.

Yes, we know you can't help your eyes…we understand that no matter who we think we are, there is always someone out there who looks better than us—but we DO NOT want to hear you point that out. Yes, most women will say they don't care if their guy compliments another female, but don't get carried away. No woman wants you pointing out all of the "one-ups" some other woman has on her. Keep it to yourself.

## 7. That you just want to be friends.

This is another one of those things that we women say we can handle, but in all reality, it hurts. We generally figure out way early on whether or not we "like-like" you and as soon as we do figure that out, we're doing everything we can to make sure the feeling is mutual. So, for you to come out and say that you just want to be friends?—yeah, dagger through the heart. Seriously. Nevertheless, I'd much rather you go ahead and tell me that than to lead me on, so kudos to you if you're man enough to let her know how you feel.

## 8. That you're not ready for commitment.

Just like saying you just want to be friends, this is another dagger through the heart of the woman who has been being faithful to you in hopes of some long-term commitment from you. When you say you're not ready for commitment all she hears is that she just wasted her time and she's not good enough for you. Again, this is one of those things that although it hurts to hear, it needs to be said if that's truly the way you feel.

# 13

# 5 Reasons Summer Is The Best Time To Get Into A Relationship

I know that right now you're probably thinking…why the hell would I get in a relationship during the longest break I have? But I've got the answers. Here are 5 reasons summertime is the BEST time to get in a relationship. Let's get into it!

## 1. You'll have first dibs on the best picks.

Look on the bright side. If you're mature enough to let a summer relationship appeal to you, you need to realize just how many people will not see the potential in it. Which means there are fewer idiots taking up all the quality mates out there. There are tons of people who are always looking for love, most times it's just in the wrong places. This summer find them and watch the relationship flourish between the two of you in ways you wouldn't imagine.

## 2. Summer dates are cheaper than dates in colder months.

When the weather is beautiful, there are so many activities the two of you can do that are way less pricey than when it's cold outside. From picnics to fishing trips, outdoor adventures are pretty much endless within the summertime. Instead of having to waste all of your money on going to restaurants, movies, and other indoor activities during the winter, get creative and take advantage of the great summer date opportunities out there.

## 3. Summer relationships move slower than relationships during 'cuffing season'.

One thing I'm sure you've noticed is that when the weather gets colder, people want to hook-up or build relationships a little more than when it was summertime. Sometimes, this makes a relationship move a lot faster than it should. When it's summertime, the both of you are likely to spend quality time together, but the both of you will also spend time with your friends or take trips away from each other. There are a lot of other differences you will experience, but this on it's own will allow the relationship to progress at a slower, more productive rate.

## 4. The sex is hotter.

Sweat is sexy. With all the adventure the two of you will embark on during the summer, the two of you are bound to have more crazy-wild, passionate sex (in some interesting places). Not that this can't happen in the winter, but trust me...summer sex is the BEST sex.

## 5. Summer relationships are more fun overall.

Gorgeous weather. Less stress. The adventurous crush. Amazing sex. I mean, if these don't sound like good reasons to give summer love a try then I've just wasted my time. Summer relationships allow you to experience your partner in a completely different way. The both of you will be in a great mood the majority of the time. You'll get to know each other better over the long summer nights. You'll experience the creative, adventurous side of one another. You'll party together. You'll have amazing sex—and ultimately, that's the recipe to a great relationship!

Don't miss out on the opportunity to enjoy this summer with someone special. They're waiting for you.

# 14

# How To Avoid A Bad First Date

What gets me the most about being single is that I love going on dates! Don't you? I do all that I can to make sure my date has a great time. Yes, even if that means paying. I think the only bad thing about going on dates is that just because you enjoyed it doesn't mean that your date did. Over time, I've both experienced and observed some really, really bad dates. So, here's a little insight on how to avoid having a bad first date. Let's get into it, shall we?

## Pre-date Signs

For some reason, we don't pay as much attention to the signs we see from the person we've invited on a date before we ever go on a date. If you choose to pay attention you can get a lot of information from it. For example, what time did they arrive? If they were eager to get to you, they are probably really excited about going out with you for the first time. Were they really late? Sure, there is a possibility that there was major traffic or some other reason for their tardiness, but normally it just means there was no sense of urgency to getting to this date. "Sorry, I'm late... I didn't want to come."

There's also the communication that comes before actually

getting together. Of course, one of the two of you had to invite the other on the date. Was there any contact beforehand? Maybe one of you sent a, "I'm really looking forward to seeing you tonight," text or something of that nature. Those are all big signs that they have been looking forward to inviting you out and that they're flattered you accepted. Those are signs that the date should run smoothly once it gets going.

## Once you arrive

Once the two of you arrive at whichever place chosen for your date (which hopefully is NOT the movie theater—worst first date, ever), pay attention to the way your date greets you. Also, consider the way you feel greeting them. Is there a natural attraction already present? Perhaps as soon as you see your date you start to think about how great they look just to go out with you, better yet, maybe you decide to tell them how great they look? Butterflies or mild nervousness is also a good sign. Keep in mind that I said mild nervousness. Meaning the kind of nervousness you get when having the opportunity to go out on a date with a crush, not the kind of nervousness that keeps you from making eye contact or speaking clearly or loudly.

What about etiquette? For us ladies is your date opening the door for you? Maybe he pulled out your chair? And to you gents, how is she dressed? If your mom walked into the place you two are having your date, would she meet a rose or a weed? I know you men may not think about it, but the way a lady dresses for your first night out says a lot about the kind of lady she is (or is not).

## During the date

Of course, the most important time to evaluate how your date is going is during the date—after the initial nervousness has worn off and before the food comes. It's during the down time that you two are sitting a table, looking each other in the eye trying to think of things to say. Gents, a kind gesture is to suggest some things on the menu that you enjoy if you've already eaten there. Ladies, this is a nice gesture for us to do, as well, but be careful because it can also come off as being a bit pushy—which we have a tendency of doing to guys, whether we realize it or not. Also, consider ordering a drink for her if she drinks alcohol. Start by asking her what her favorite drink is and then suggest a few drinks that would compliment her taste based on her answer. This is a nice trick in the book for us, too, ladies.

Pay attention to the vibe you two have created. Is it comfortable? Do you feel relaxed and happy to be on a date with the person you're with? Is your mind completely engaged or entirely distracted? This is important. Whatever vibe you two have going is already sending signs to both of you about whether or not you two will be going out again. Also consider how deep your conversation is. No, you don't need to tell your date your deepest darkest secrets on the first night out, but hopefully your conversation excels beyond simple questions like your favorite food or color. You want to leave enough on the table that makes your date feel like you were comfortable telling them who you are, but also being careful not to leave it all out there so that your date is hungry to learn more about you.

What about body language? If your date is a female, some ways to know she is enjoying herself are relaxed shoulders, crossed legs that are pointing in your direction, and a bright smile, of course. Some women are also really likely to play with their hair when having a good time. Also, if she actually laughs instead of just smiling…you're doing great. For the gents, from what I can see, being engaged in the conversation is a good sign because unlike us women, men aren't always big on open conversation. Also, eye contact, offering another round of drinks or dessert (in efforts to make the date last longer) are also telltale signs that he is enjoying your company. Ladies, we can also offer a second round of drinks or dessert in order to let him know you'd like to stay a little while longer and that you're enjoying your time.

## Post-date Signs

Hopefully you haven't seen your dates phone until the end of the date only to find that the two of you spent hours of enjoyable time together. I hate when my date texts while on our date, but that's just me. Anyway, the follow-up is very important. When you two are saying your goodbyes, it is just as important to pay attention to the signs being given here. Is your date eager to get outta there? Or maybe they are trying everything in their power to linger and hang out a little while longer? Did you two feel comfortable giving each other a goodbye hug instead of the awkward 'handshake/hug/um, what are you doing?' Did the two of you talk about or plan another date before leaving the first one?

Also, pay attention to the interaction the two of you have once you've already parted ways. Maybe your date asked you to text them when you made it home safely? That's a good sign, but it also takes initiative from you to actually let them know you made it. Maybe you ride home thinking about how much you enjoyed yourself and call your date when you make it in to let them know that. The follow-up is to me the most important because it is what will lead the two of you to having more dates in the future and to hopefully pursuing more.

For the most part, I referred to the first date taking place over dinner, which I find highly appropriate, but you don't have to be that simple. Either way, you want to make sure you pay attention to all parts of the date. In my opinion, these are the makings of a great first date and more importantly, a great first impression. Good luck!

# 15

# How To (Respectfully) Date Multiple Men At Once

Before you lose your cool, dating multiple men and fucking multiple men are, indeed, two very different things.

The type of person who can respectfully date around is the type of person who knows what they're looking for and has no intentions of settling on that. Before shopping online, you read reviews to make sure the product is worth your money, right? Dating multiple men at once is very similar to that process. Here's how to respectfully date multiple men at once.

## 1. Weigh all of your options.

When you're dating around, it's okay to compare the men you're seeing. Speaking from personal experience, when I've dated multiple men at once there was always one who did something that the others didn't do. Who did I like best? Which man had the best qualities? Were those qualities anything like what I said I was looking for in a man? All of these things were questions I considered while dating multiple men at once. My point being, it was to weigh my options—not to just see how many men I could juggle at one time.

## 2. Find the one with the best value.

This might not sound very nice to some, but it's honest. When you weigh all of your options you are choosing the man who provides the most value to you. Who do you see yourself building a lasting relationship with. You can't take them all, so you need to find the one with the best value. Keep in mind that the highest price doesn't necessarily mean they'll have the best value. Don't be bamboozled by a man who will buy you anything you want. Most times those type of men are so fucking shallow and insecure it's insane. Just FYI. Instead, think of your life and try to determine which man would bring the most value to it. Who supports your goals? Who makes you laugh? Who offers you valuable conversation?

## 3. Choose one man.

Like I've already said, this is not about being selfish. You only get to keep one man. This is why it's important to take the first two steps so seriously. You really need to spend quality time getting to know the men you're considering so that when it's time to make a decision you can make one confidently.

## 4. Make the best decision the first time around.

When you follow all of the previously mentioned steps, it's not hard to make the best decision the very first time. You end up choosing the man who provides the best value in your life. You end up choosing the man who has great qualities. You end up choosing the best man for you. When we date one guy at a time sometimes you end up going through that "trial and error" stage where you enter countless meaningless relationships that all could have been avoided by dating around and testing the waters first.

Time is precious and waits for no man (or woman). If you're capable of dating multiple men discreetly and without having sex with them during the process, I encourage you to do so! You will be able to pick the best man, who has the best value, the very first time around—and there's absolutely nothing wrong with weighing more than one option to find him.

# 16

# What You're Really Saying To The Chick(s) You Let Crash At Your Place

From college and even now, spending the night has always been kind of a big deal. I mean, be honest, you don't usually just let anybody spend the night. Most women are more likely to let you stay over if you want to and there really is no miscommunication about you being a "special someone" if you gain that privilege. You men, though...I can't say the same. I believe that you allowing a women to spend the night definitely sends a message whether you intended it to or not. Here's what you're really saying to the chick(s) you let crash at your place. Let's get into it.

## One-Nighters

Whether you realize it and don't care or you don't realize it at all, a one-nighter usually doesn't feel good to a female. Usually the only motivation behind a one-nighter is sex. Really and truly, the only times a female is okay with this type of sleepover is if her goal was sex and doesn't plan on seeing you again or if she's feeling confident that there will be another invitation in the (very) near future. She won't really get her hopes up high, but you should either. The one-nighter type of chick is a heartbreaker. She's not the type to cuddle after she gets off and she definitely won't be in the kitchen making breakfast when you wake up—she might not even be there when you wake up. Be careful, big guy.

## Every Other Day-ers

Don't confuse this with sleeping over consecutively; although intentions may be the same…when she's staying over multiple times a week, she'll still be sensitive to the time you two are spending together—but she'll be a lot less likely to leave her stuff behind and engage in the "playing house" actions so soon. This is a much more comfortable situation for the both of you when you're both feeling each other, but things haven't gotten too serious yet. At this point, when she's sleeping over it's not just about sex. She really wants to spend quality time with you and more than likely enjoys falling asleep in your arms and waking up to your morning breath. If you've reached this stage and it's still just about the sex for you, it's probably best to let the poor girl go.

## Frequent, Consecutive Nights

When you allow a female to stay over consecutive nights, DO NOT believe her when she says it means nothing—shit has definitely gotten real. To her, it may not be a huge deal, but it definitely means something. Y'all are damn near shacking up! Whether making a relationship between the two of you seem closer in reach (if she doesn't already see it as a reality) or if she's proving to herself that she takes precedence over any other female in your life—it means something to her. This is when you'll start seeing a lot of the "playing house" actions. She'll be cooking without being asked or leaving clothes at your place instead of bringing a 'spend-the-night bag' every time she comes around and she'll probably be wearing your clothes as night clothes just to name a few. Ultimately, to her, it's safe to say that things are getting pretty serious between the two of you. You may even find that she's wanting to be at the house even when you're not there. Again, at this point, sex has nothing to do with her presence there. She's there for you. You may not have realized it, but once the two of you reach this stage…the end goal is more than likely to be in a relationship with you which is hopefully the same for you.

Another motive a female may have behind staying over so much is to make sure that no one else is staying over! Don't be blind to that fact either. Not all girls are looking for a relationship, some girls just want to milk you for as much as they can while they have the chance. So, don't be naïve to the fact that you men can get played just like a female can.

## 17

# How To Tell If You're Getting Played By A Woman With Serious Game

I think many of you have forgotten that women can play the game even better than men. With that, I want to talk about some of the signs that you're dating a woman with no intentions of getting serious—in other words, I want to tell you how to spot the ways women use men to get what they want without committing. To keep things simple…when in doubt, get out! If she has intentions of pursuing a relationship with you, you'll know. Trust me. A woman with game is a dangerous thing, so beware of the devil in a new dress. Here's how to tell if you're getting played by a woman with serious game.

### If you call, she'll answer—but she sure as hell isn't calling you first.

This is how it all started. You saw her and thought, "man, I've got to get her…" you talked her into giving you her phone number and she might have even seem interested. You go to call her and maybe she picks up the first time, maybe she doesn't (because she doesn't recognize the number), but when you finally get in contact with her, the sparks that you just knew were there when you met her seem to have dulled out. You remind her of who you are, she engages a little more in conversation and finally you two are off to (what you think is) a good start. From here, in order to see her again, you ask her out on a date and (reluctantly) she accepts. You've been hooked.

## You go out on dates, but you're not "dating."

Free drinks or free food is always an incentive to go out on a date. This is initially how most women get over on you gents. A woman who has no intentions of dating you will still go out on all kinds of dates with you just to get out of the house without having to spend her own money. Usually the dates are in places that the two of you aren't very likely to be seen in, like dinner in a back booth or the movies, instead of a night out on the town for all to see. If you find yourself always offering to take her out, it's not usually a good sign of progression. If she were into you, she'd suggest dates and even pay sometimes.

## You pay for EVERYTHING.

I highly doubt that I am the first person to tell you this. Women love money. It doesn't really matter who it comes from. If you're willing to pick up the ticket no matter where the two of you go, she'll keep you around. If you buy her whatever she wants, she'll keep you around. If she knows she can call you to get a few extra bucks, she'll keep you around. If you pay her bills, she'll keep you around...but none of this means she has any intention of committing herself to you—at all. If you're doing any of these things without reciprocity—you're digging your own grave. And let's be clear about one little thing...SEX IS NOT THE APPROPRIATE RECIPROCATION.

## She uses 'the cookie' to eat the cake.

I know it feels amazing and can be wildly invigorating, but gents...you have got to stop holding so much value to sex. And before you start denying that you do this, I'm not talking about sex with any ol' gal...I'm talking about sex with that girl. I'm talking about sex with the girl you have sex with and decide you want to be the only one having sex with her. Sex is not money. Sex is not love. Sex does not hold any additional value besides reaching a moment of ecstasy—and that's only if you really know what you're doing. A woman who has no intention of dating you, but wants to keep taking advantage of your money or other things, has no problem opening up her legs to make you think everything is all good between the two of you.

## She's two different people alone with you and in public.

You may be feeling a little confused because you're thinking to yourself..."we don't have sex...we make love." Or maybe you two have really intimate conversations when you're alone and you guys cuddle all the time, but let me break it down. If you two can do all of these things in the privacy of your own home, that's one thing. When you two can do the same things no matter who's looking...that is a whole other ball game. If she tends to get a little more "reserved" when the two of you are in public, it could be because she doesn't want anyone thinking you two are more than friends. If it's okay to kiss at the house, but you can't hold hands while walking in the mall—she's playing you, buddy.

## She just wants you to "be patient" with her.

Patience. A woman who has no intentions of committing to you, but still wants to reap the benefits you bring will continue to make you think that with time, the two of you will finally live happily ever after. This is not true. Women know very soon whether or not they want to pursue a relationship with their partner of choosing. If she wanted to commit, you would know so. When she says she needs time or wants you to be patient, it is generally just a way to keep you around without having to give you what you ultimately want from her—commitment.

## You're always introduced as a friend or by your name.

Unfortunately, after all this time, although the two of you do go out together, you're still being introduced as her friend or worse...just as your name. Neither of these introductions allow her friends to confirm their assumption that you two might be more than friends no matter how many times they have seen you together because the bottom line is, if you were somebody…she would have said so.

So, how long is too long to wait on the commitment, you ask? I'd say depending on how many of the previously mentioned signs you've seen, you've already waited too long, but if you need a number…I'd say a month and a half, two months of no real reciprocity or intention is more than enough reason to get outta there. Don't get played, gents. The right one is out there somewhere!

# 18

# 5 Telltale Signs That You're More Into Them Than They're Into You

Don't feel bad about liking someone more than they like you. For someone like me, I always like my crushes more than they like me at first. I'm a lover. It's what I do. Sometimes it just feels like you like that person more than they like you, but there are some subtle ways of telling as well. Here are five telltale signs that you're more into it them than they're into you.

## 1. You hear from them, but only if you text or call first.

It's not that you can't reach them when you try. It's just that if you don't text or call them first, you wouldn't hear from them. They could honestly let days go without hitting you up at all. I've been here before and I'll tell you the truth—I felt really fucking stupid. I don't really advise that you give your time to anybody who can go days without thinking of you or talking to you, but that's just me.

## 2. Communication only happens if you drive the conversation.

If you're not constantly starting the conversation with a lead question that pretty much requires a response, they wouldn't say a whole lot to you. In fact, they're often very quiet and only say generic things like "oh okay" or "that's crazy" as a response every time you say something.

## 3. You spend time together, but only if you initiate the plans.

You can come over to their place, but they probably aren't going out of their way to come and see you. You guys can go hang out somewhere, but the invite would have to come from you. See what I'm getting at here? Only when you initiate the plans, does this person follow through. Spontaneous adventures never come with their name next to sender, that's for sure.

## 4. They don't introduce you to any close family or friends.

Never underestimate what it means to meet someone's friends and family. These are the people who usually encourage that person to buckle down or let you go, depending on their feelings about you. Either way, it shouldn't be taken lightly. It is also a huge sign that this person likes where things are headed with you and thinks it's important that you are introduced to the people they love. It doesn't always happen right away, so be patient, but if it doesn't happen at all, that usually is a message on it's own.

## 5. They only do for you because you do things for them.

I don't take kindly to "tit-for-tat" actions. Don't do me any favors. If you do something for me, I want you to do it because you want to—not because feel like you have to. Anybody who makes you feel bad because they did something for you is not the type of person you want to invest your time in. If it's that hard for them to do nice things for you that is definitely a sign that you are not the one they'd like to be seeing too much more of in the the future.

## 19

# 7 Responses To "What Are We?" That Let You Know Exactly WTF Is Up

Have you ever been in a relationship with someone and later realized that you're the only one who considers the two of you actually being "in a relationship?" I've learned that many people steer clearing of defining the relationship they have with someone and instead, try to tag on words like "talking" or "dating around." As in, "there's no commitment between us, but I don't want you to 'talk' to anyone else." There are several excuses or reasons for why someone does this, but don't fool yourself—you deserve clarity. If you are in a relationship or doing "relationship things" with someone and you've never defined the situation, it's time to get some answers. Here are seven responses to "what are we?" that let you know exactly where things stand with you two. Let's get into it!

## 1. "I don't want to complicate what we have."

"You're special to me and you know that, but I don't want to complicate what we have by putting a title on it." If putting a title on your situationship will cause complications, that is a very clear sign that commitment is only a goal for one of you.

## 2. "We're buddies."

Abort mission—like, now. This is such a huge sign of disrespect to me. You're not just one of his male friends, and this honestly…this is just a nonchalant way of telling you that there is no potential of a committed relationship for the two of you in sight.

## 3. "Seriously…we're just friends."

This response is typically made by you when you're explaining to others (who are tired of you two dragging things out) that you're just friends when everyone knows you two should be more. You're trying to convince others that (even though you two would be perfect together) you aren't going to embark on a romantic relationship. Sure, you could be worried about risking the friendship, but in all honesty, you know that you both should be more than friends as well! Go ahead, take the risk!

## 4. "Soon, but not now."

"I'm just not ready for a relationship right now. To me, hearing this is risky. It all depends on the person as to whether or not you can believe there is light at the end of this tunnel. Some people use this excuse to keep you around, but they never make that leap and "soon" never comes. It doesn't happen that way in all cases though. Some people do need time to prioritize or handle themselves emotionally before getting involved in a new relationship. Again, trusting this response is all on the person it's coming from.

## 5. "You know I'll always care about you."

You two may have been 'involved' for quite some time, but still that commitment has not been made. As long as you two have been a "thing," it has been serious and the two of you have developed real feelings for each other. Shitty thing is, as deep as those feelings are, you still aren't getting anywhere with them. "You know they'll always care about you," but commitment (at least to you) is not the end goal for them.

## 6. "What are you doing later?"

This is the person who dances around the question to begin with. You might not want to admit it, but you know exactly who I'm talking about. You know good and well nothing will come from this. In fact, they treat you like a booty call: only reaching out when they want to sleep with you and even that is pretty scarce. You know so well what the two of you are that you don't even bother asking because the honest answer will make you feel even more stupid than you do now. Move on, baby.

## 7. "I thought you knew that we were just hooking up."

You hear from this person a little more than the "WYD later?"

type, but still you're just hooking up. There really isn't anything exclusive or promising about the relationship. In fact, the term "hook-up" generally applies that it's a casual, nonexclusive type of relationship—meaning you and four others are probably expecting the same commitment from this one person who has zero intentions of committing to any of you.

All in all, if you are committing yourself to someone who hasn't committed themselves to you, then you're selling yourself short. You're a pink Starburst, remember? You are the shit. You deserve to be treated as such…gain some clarity and if you get any of the following responses in return—believe them the first time!

# 20

# How Long Should I Wait For Someone To "Be Ready" To Commit?

I read a meme on Facebook that said, "No matter how much he likes you, if you're still single, he doesn't like you that much." At first, I agreed. Then I didn't. Then I realized that really there was an underlying question that would make or break this confusion for me. He could really like you, but he could be waiting on the right time or he could be the kind of person this meme is implying—meaning he could just be full of shit. The real question here is how long should I wait for someone to "be ready" to commit to me?

I think I acknowledge pretty often that I don't know everything. In fact, there are a ton of things I don't know—but relationship advice just so happens to be my "thing." Just to be clear on that. Now, based on their reasoning behind why they aren't "ready" to commit to you will let you know whether or not you should keep waiting. Personally, I can't think of very many things going on in a person's life that getting into a committed relationship would hinder, but that doesn't mean it couldn't happen. That would be for you to determine.

It's okay to embark on a new thing and take it slow in the

beginning as long as eventually you want to be committed. When you let taking things "slow" substitute for any actual progress towards commitment, you're playing yourself. That is how you get stuck in a situationship. Establish the relationship. It's fine to take some time and take things slow, but always establish the relationship. As long as you're making progress towards being in a relationship, you're good.

So, how long is too long to wait for them to be ready to make a commitment? You've waited too long when you start to feel like your time is being wasted. Naturally, most of us have a pretty good idea of when someone is trying to deceive us. Trust your gut. If you feel like there's no light at the end of the tunnel, turn around now. There's no need to keep walking only to end up at a dark dead-end.

# 21

# The Secret To Every Woman's Heart

The secret to every woman's heart. As complex and/or annoying as us woman can seem, we're really very simple. All of our lives, we are told that the way to your heart is through your stomach…is that true? Either way, I promise you that once you finish this, we women will make a lot more sense to you then we probably ever have…so, let's get into it!

First, I want you to think of the things all women have in common. Yes, all women. That means it can't be fashion, it can't be hairstyles, and it can't even be the attraction of men.. It's not so easy, is it? So, I'll tell you.

## AMBITION.

I don't know a single woman in the world who doesn't want something for herself. It may not be the ideal job or the ideal lifestyle, but still she has a goal and her eye is on that prize. So what's the secret?

The secret to every woman's heart is to support her ambitions.

There is nothing more attractive about a man than his willingness to support not just a woman's ambition, but anyone's.

If you think about it, the kind of men women usually voice as their "dream guy" is one who is a business owner, role model, or some type of leader at least. It's because we enjoy a man who is strong enough to lead, passionate enough to help, and bold enough to show it.

As common as it may seem, it is not an everyday situation that we find a man who supports our thoughts, ideas, and visions. I guess I should have mentioned earlier that I'm not really talking about the secret to getting the woman but more so showing you how to stand out and gain a place in her life that really won't fade. We won't turn our backs on someone who supports us—in anyway, but especially someone who supports our ambitions. We need it. We are far more likely to foster the friendship or relationship because we need that support. Especially when it's coming from a strong man.

Ask that woman what her plans for life are. Ask that woman what her goals are. Ask that woman what steps she has already taken to get closer to achieving those goals. Ask that woman what else she needs to do and if she needs help getting there. After that, KEEP UP WITH HER ABOUT THOSE THINGS. Hold her accountable for the goals she's put before herself and all the things she said she would do to achieve them. Praise her for her accomplishments, but get on her case a little bit when she's losing her drive. These are the foolproof strategies.

You'll find that naturally, she'll share her thoughts with you and keep you included every step of the way because she's gaining a lot from your friendship. She'll definitely grow fond of your care and interest in her goals and plans. That speaks volumes.

You want to blow a woman's mind? Show her much you appreciate and support a woman with ambition.

# 22

# What It's Like To Date A Woman On Her Shit

Confident, beautiful, and on her shit. There isn't really another way to describe the woman who is about her business. Dating an ambitious woman should be your goal, fellas. Sure, I'll go ahead and say it…she might seem like a bitch at first, but she's just serious about where she's going in life. There are a ton of benefits as to why this kind of woman should be the lady you're looking for, but I'll just point out a few to get you started. Here's what it's really like to date a woman who is about her business. Let's get into it!

## She has her shit together, so save the bull for someone else.

You aren't going to pull the wool over her eyes. She takes herself seriously and won't allow anyone to waste her time. Nine times out of ten, she's already kind of skeptical about investing time into something new anyway. Her time is valuable and she's tired of wasting it on men with nothing to offer, but sex and games. When you date a woman who is about her business, you should value her time just as much as she has. If you're still about games, she's definitely not the woman you need in your life.

## She wants to be in control, but if you're a strong man she'll release the reins a bit.

A woman who is about her business naturally takes control. She can't help it; it's who she is. Although she is used to controlling situations, when you're man enough, a woman is willing to let you take the lead. You have to make her see that you can handle leading her though. If you're intimidated by her alone, she won't trust that you are strong enough to lead her. If you can show her that you respect the fact that she is a strong, independent woman, BUT you're the man and are capable of taking the lead—trust me, she won't fight you about it. In fact, it's a major turn on for a man to be able to put his foot down without stepping on his woman. Master that.

## She's on her Ps and Qs, so she'll expect you to be the same way.

You gotta come correct. You gotta have something to offer. A woman who is about her business isn't perfect, but she's striving to be. She wants you to be a reflection of her and vice versa. She wants you to be confident, charismatic, and everything else she feels that she brings to the table.

## She has a serious work ethic, but she also enjoys letting her hair down.

All work and no play isn't good for anybody. Yes, a woman who is about her business works hard, but she plays even harder. She won't allow a good time to jeopardize her quality of work or her ability to get it done, but when all the work is done she is definitely down to have a good time. This is a good thing. A woman who is about her business is the best of both worlds. She's serious about what matters, but she's an adventurous risk-taker—even in bed.

## She wants you to work for her, but she's worth it.

At the end of the day, a woman who is about her business may be strong and independent, but she's still a woman. She needs affection. She wants to experience romance. She wants to feel needed. She will challenge you to see if you can deliver on those things—but here's the catch—without making her feel weak. This is why her initial reactions will seem uninterested or unimpressed because she doesn't want you to see her being too soft. So, yeah...she'll make you chase her, but she's worth it. I promise.

## Once you prove yourself, she's yours forever.

A woman who is about her business values her time. It's one of her most valuable assets. That being said, once she realizes that you haven't wasted her time and you can handle being her counterpart, she will respect everything that you two have built and will build. She's loyal. She won't let anyone or anything come between what she's now investing her heart and time into. She won't give up on you guys easily. She'll always want to solve whatever problems you two come up against. That also means though, that if you break her heart you had better be ready to experience hell, buddy. Hell hath no fury like an [ambitious] woman scorned.

Are you man enough to handle her? Sure you are! Now, get out there and make someone happy!

## 23

# Do It For The Gram: 3 Reasons Why Your Girlfriend Wants You To Show Her Off

Although it might seem like overkill, I don't know any woman that doesn't desire a man who wouldn't shout his love for her from the rooftops. No, social media outlets aren't necessarily the rooftops, but it's public enough for her to feel appreciated for all to see. Social media is just an example though—it's about the easiest option there is. If posting pictures all the time on social media isn't your thing, that's no big deal at all. That is not the only way to show off your woman. You can show your woman off by introducing her to your closest friends and family. You can show your woman off by presenting meaningful gifts to her, demonstrating that you appreciate her. You can even show your woman off simply by holding her hand in public. And, no. You're not "doing it for other people." You're doing it for her—just to be clear on that. Like I said, there are a number of different ways to show your woman off. "Is this really necessary?" You might be asking. Here are three simple reasons to show your woman off every chance you get. Let's get into it.

## 1. Pride

More often than not when we think of pride it is usually used to describe someone who is too prideful. I'm not using pride in that context here. I'm talking about the deep feeling of satisfaction that comes from your personal accomplishment to have embarked on a relationship with the woman you admire and have chosen to be with. I'm talking about being damn happy about finally bagging the one you've been wanting all this time. No matter how you choose to show your woman off, one of the reasons you should choose to do so is because you're proud to be with her—no matter who sees. Also, this isn't about just being proud of how she looks. It's more importantly being proud of who she is—her ambitions, her goals, her values—her heart.

## 2. Joy

"Be with someone who gives you the same feeling of excitement as seeing your food coming to the table in a restaurant." …or however that saying goes is a perfect example of what I'm trying to say here. Another ridiculously simple reason to show your woman off is because she makes you happy—and not just any kind of happy; she makes you the 'my favorite team won with a three-point shot at the buzzer' kind of happy. The interesting thing about this reason for showing off your woman is that men are highly likely to feel this way, but men are very hesitant in showing it. I get it. You don't want everybody in your business (and you probably don't want to seem 'whipped'), but again, you're not doing this for anyone but her. What other people think doesn't matter. I mean, she is that special, right? Show your woman off because of the divine happiness she provides you.

## 3. Security

Last, but not least, show your woman off as a sense of security—for both of you. When you show your woman off because you're proud to be with her and because of how much joy she brings to your life, you're showing her that you're secure in the relationship. You're also showing her that she doesn't have any outside threats to worry about. I'm not saying that temptation won't arise because all women know a faithful man is a desperate and jealous woman's target, but she won't be worried about that kind of woman because of the man who is by her side. That's what it's all about...TRUST.

When you show your woman off for these simple reasons, you're giving her even more reason to trust you. You can build a dynasty with trust. You can reach the end of time with trust. The options are truly endless when the two of you have trust. Don't let your worry for what other people might think stop you from showing the woman you are building with that she means the world to you and that you're proud to call her yours. If that's not reason enough to show your woman off, I can almost guarantee you that things will become a lot more adventurous between the two of you on dates, in bed, and in everything else you do when you show her off for these three reasons! When she's happy...you'll be happy too.

# 24

# How Being A Mom Made Me More Desirable To Men

Having a baby is no small task. Being able to wear pregnancy as a single mother is not an easy appearance to put forth, but with the right attitude it is completely possible. Although my circumstances weren't ideal, I was genuinely happy with the thought of having a child. It showed. Along with my genuine happiness for an opportunity to raise life, I believe there are a few other things that come with being a mom that made me more desirable to men. Before you sign off, hear me out.

When I found out I was pregnant one of my first thoughts were, "Well, there goes any chance of me being in a relationship any time soon." I think other single mothers can probably relate. Little did I know that I was very wrong. I'll admit that some men just wanted to try me because they heard pregnant sex is awesome, but that's neither here nor there. There are many who have been attracted by the transformation my daughter has allowed me to experience. Here's how being a mom made me more desirable to men. Let's get into it.

## Being a mom made me responsible.

Yes, I was responsible before being a mom, but now there's a different sense of responsibility that I feel. When you have a baby (if you know what's best for you), you get your shit together—to keep it real. You tie all your loose ends (or cut them off). You get all your ducks in a row. You focus. This is a desirable trait to find in any individual, but it is definitely one of the transformations I feel made me more desirable to men.

## Being a mom made me unapologetically chase God.

Not that I didn't already have a relationship with God, but now I'm so hungry for Him that I can hardly explain it. A lot of people probably wouldn't admit it, but I'm not afraid to say that before my daughter, I allowed many things to distract me and even scare me out of making sure every man who tried to pursue me knew that if He didn't want a stronger relationship with God then there was no possibility of a lasting one with me. It might seem harsh to some, but for those who desire the kind of relationship that I do with the Lord...I know it makes sense.

## Being a mom made me get rid of my bad habits.

*Of course* being a mom allowed me to get rid of my bad habits. It goes without saying how much your life changes when you have a baby, but the things you let go of while being pregnant don't just come back after baby is here—and that is a phenomenal thing. Your social bad habits, 'small' bad habits, bad habits you didn't even realize you had—all of those things basically make you cringe at the thought of doing them now that you're a parent. This makes for a much brighter, more positive you and that is definitely desirable to men.

## Being a mom made me see who my real friends are.

I don't think us women realize that men care about what type of people we consider friends. The friends we choose are, indeed, a reflection of us. Personally, I think men are much better at friendship than woman, but that is just my personal opinion. Regardless, I know for a fact that men care about who we choose to call friend. The minute you announce your pregnancy you start to see what friends are truly your friends. You'll learn that some 'friends' can't be friends with the sober, mom version of you. It's unfortunate, but it's true. When you do realize who your friends are, it's a great feeling. It's just another one of those things that makes for a brighter, better version of you and as I said before, that 'you' is much more desirable than the you that you used to be.

## Being a mom made me more mature.

Who doesn't love a mature individual? Even if you thought you were mature before being a mom, you will soon realize that your maturity has developed on an entirely new level. Your maturity is what allows you to experience all of the changes I've just previously explained. Furthermore, that maturity allows you to see how marvelous those transformations really are. It's a real eye opener. Of course, any man is attracted to a mature woman—at least all the men I know.

## Being a mom made me take myself seriously.

Being a mom made me take myself seriously. I had to type it twice just to stress how true this is. I take myself so seriously now, it's scary—for some people. I AM A MOTHER. I don't have time for anything that is not making me into a better woman and mother for my little girl. That meant I had to look myself in the mirror and tell myself just that. Before anybody else could take me seriously, I had to do it. Now that I have reached that realization, I present myself in exactly that light. In other words, men know they can't approach me with bullshit and I think any "real man" can appreciate that. It's a challenge and that is desirable.

## Being a mom made me a woman.

Straight like that. No matter how "grown" I thought I was before, being a mom has really made a woman out of me. The countless lessons I have learned in just this short time proves to me day-in and day-out that I was just a child before all of this. I have never felt more woman in all of my life. Powerful. Fearless. Wise. Hungry. Proud. Confident. I could go on for days. I don't know a man who wouldn't want to describe his woman as anything less.

So you may agree with me and then again, you might not. Either way, I've noticed a huge difference in myself and the type of men who have reached out to me since bringing my daughter into this world. Whether it was to tell me how beautiful motherhood looks on me or to talk about the possibility of a relationship between the two of us, being a mom has definitely made me more desirable to (the right kind of) men.

## 25

# 15 Signs Your Relationship Is On The Right Track

Dating is risky, but sometimes you get lucky and stumble upon a great woman or man. I'm not saying that it's guaranteed that things will last forever, but if you see some of these signs within your relationship now, then I think it's safe to say that your relationship is on the right track! Let's get into it!

## 1. You're paying attention to the small things that matter to one another.

It's the small things—the *simple* things—that really show how much someone means to you.

## 2. You're patient with one another.

Love takes patience. It takes the willingness to know that things are going to take time to be where you need it to be. You have to be willing to stick that out, together.

## 3. You willingly and openly communicate with one another about everything.

You're not asking how each other's day has been because "It's the right thing to do," you're asking because you genuinely care about how their day has been. You talk to each other like you're best friends. That's love.

## 4. You don't like saying no to one another, but you will if it is necessary.

You're spoiled and you know it. Both of you hate having to tell the other "no" because you only want to see each other happy—but, if it's necessary, you can say no when the time calls for it.

## 5. You're willing to make sacrifices for one another.

If you're not willing to make sacrifices for the person you're in a relationship with... Get. Out. NOW.

## 6. You're making a conscious effort to improve yourself for them (in any area).

They just make you want to be a better person. Even if it's something as small as not cursing anymore, they make you want to improve yourself.

## 7. Sexual activity is deep and emotional.

It's never just sex with you two. You make love. To be honest, sex is not about your pleasure, but more about theirs.

## 8. You don't seek outside attention.

The need for social media and the popularity that comes with it slowly but surely goes away. You'll even find that talking and texting other people on the phone is less desirable. The only person's attention you need and want is your partners.

## 9. You don't mind going out of your way to make one another happy.

You'll do whatever it takes to make sure your partner is happy. In fact, it doesn't even seem like you're going above and beyond to you, but other people might bring that to your attention. Again, you just want to do what you can to make and keep them happy.

## 10. You respect one another with or without being in each other's presence.

Whether they're standing right next to you or in Timbuktu—respect is not an option. You don't disrespect your partner or your relationship and you don't allow anyone else to disrespect your partner or your relationship—point blank, period.

## 11. You talk about each other to your close friends and family.

They're special to you. They bring out the best in you. These things make you want to tell your close friends and family all about the person responsible for the new glow you've been sporting lately.

## 12. You've met each other's close family and friends.

Not only do you talk about them with your close family and friends, but you make it a point to have them meet one another. I think meeting the family is very underplayed with Millennials. Meeting the family is a really big deal!

## 13. You show and tell one another how much you mean to each other.

No matter how you choose to show each other or what words you choose to express it, you both make it a priority to display that love and affection as often as possible. Saying "I love you" is easy, normal, and frequent for the two of you.

## 14. Talking about the future isn't off-limits.

If you can't talk about the future with your partner, chances are there isn't one in sight for one of you. It's important to know that your partner is comfortable thinking about the possibility of your future with them.

## 15. You're planning for a future together.

You don't just talk about a future together, but you're making progress towards making it a reality. You're planning to save, thinking about where you two want to start a family—you're making a plan to spend your future together.

## 26

# 5 Ways To Show Her You Care (That Won't Cost You Anything)

### 1. Write her a letter.

Women are emotional creatures. As such, written word touches our soul even more than spoken words. The thing about a love letter is that it lasts forever. She can always go back and read it as many times as she wants to. Although you can say sweet things, it changes a little every time. You can never get that exact moment back. Write her a letter telling her how much you love her so that she can preserve that moment for a lifetime.

### 2. Play with her hair.

Simple, yet satisfying. I have no idea what it is about a man playing in our hair, but it sure does say a lot about how you feel about us. If I had to figure it out, I'd say that it's the stillness and the quality time that comes with you playing in our hair. It's like the forehead kiss. A small gesture that really shows how much you care.

### 3. Tell her your favorite things about her.

Now you can be creative with this and it still doesn't have to cost you a dime. Don't just list off your favorite things about her, although she'd still think it was just as sweet. Find a creative way to show her all your favorite things about her; the timeless things that you'll love until the day she dies.

### 4. Eat her out.

Yes, I went there. One of the simplest ways to show her that you really care about her is to eat her out—and not just the bare minimum either. I mean really go all out, like you love it—like you love her. There is a difference and we can feel it. If you're one of those guys who still isn't "into it" then you may not be with the right person. When she's worth it, you'll get over that "eww" factor and you'll learn to love it simply because you love her. Just FYI.

### 5. Plan a future with her.

This is what it's all about. When you know that she's the one, you plan a future with her. Any woman who is committing herself to you 100% is looking for this right here. Don't let her fool you. If she's not moved by the thought of a future with you then you two should definitely see other people. That goes for you, too. You two may have already discussed some things about your future together, but actually start. Start a savings account together. Choose a song. Pick a wedding color. Whatever you two can agree is an actual 'start' to a future together.

116

## 27

# 5 Ways To Show Him You Care (That Won't Cost You Anything)

### 1. Leave him alone.

I know, at first it didn't make sense to me either. However, I've been told more often than not by several men in my life that this is one of the sweetest gifts we can give them—silence, alone time. Every man loves a little time to himself. I have no idea what they do during that time, but it's precious to them and is definitely a good way to show him you care. Make him his favorites, open his beer, turn the game on and leave him be. It'll work out in your favor.

### 2. Give him spontaneous head (and put some effort into it).

It hasn't failed me. Sure, it's a little forward for us gals, but it's the truth. I won't go into detail about how, where, or when to do it because you should leave that to your imagination, but he'll love it. Also, just like I advised the guys not to just "eat us," but to do it with a little passion—the same goes for us. Try an ice cube, use a little extra spit. Just get the job done right. Give it a shot.

## 3. Dance for him.

This one might be hit or miss for some people. I mean, if you don't like to dance I supposed this won't work for you, but it's so fun and if you've never tried it—you should. Put on something you feel sexy in and play some of those songs that make you feel like the baddest bitch in the world and let his ass have it! I mean, seriously, dance like nobody's looking! He'll find his 'private dancer' very attractive and invigorating especially if you've never done this before.

## 4. Stroke his ego.

Just do what the lyrics in Destiny's Child's "Cater To You" tell you to do. All men need their ego stroked every now and again. Remind him of how fine you think he is. Remind him of how much you appreciate what he does for you. Hopefully you're aware of the types of verbal affirmations he likes. If you're not aware of those things, that is definitely something you need to figure out quickly. Once you know just what to say to give his ego a really good stroke, lay it on thick! It wouldn't hurt to pair this up with some of the previously mentioned.

## 5. Give him a (really good) massage.

Now that you've stroked his ego, help him relax with a massage that says, "Baby, I really do appreciate you." Yes, with all the fixings—candlelight, a drink, you could even put on something pretty for him to look at (and take off) once the massage is over!

## 28

# 5 Things You Seriously Do NOT Need To Talk About In Your Relationship

When you're in a committed relationship you're supposed to be able to talk to your partner about everything, but that doesn't mean you should talk to your partner anything. Some people may not agree and if you and your partner are open about literally anything—more power to you. If your partner is anything like me though, here are five things you seriously don't need to talk about in your relationship. Let's get into it!

## 1. Poop

Yes, it's said that you're truly comfortable with your partner once you're able to fart around them, but do you really have to talk about shit? Seriously, I don't need to know when you go or where you go.

## 2. Exes

Want to drive your relationship into the ground? Talk about your ex all the time. When you talk about your ex, it's usually to compare something they did with what your current partner is doing—which is always a bad idea. They are your ex for a reason. Even if there is no bad blood between you and your ex, you shouldn't be discussing them with your current partner. This may not be such a sore subject for men (I do believe it is though), but for women it's definitely the last thing she wants to hear about.

## 3. Drama

Your drama or someone else's, it really doesn't matter. Don't discuss drama in your relationship. It's usually just a trail to a topic that you two will end up arguing about anyway. If that's not reason enough, just remember that if you're not a part of the solution, you're a part of the problem.

## 4. The Past

Timon and Pumbaa told us, "You've got to learn to put the past behind ya," and that is one of the greatest life lessons you'll ever learn. Let the past be the past. Carry the good memories in your heart, but let them chill there. No need to keep bringing them up. In all actuality, we are a lot more likely to bring up negative past experiences over positive ones anyway, so do yourself the favor and be in the moment. Focus on the present.

## 5. He Says/She Says

I don't think there is a more ridiculous argument than one that is based solely on what someone else said. This may be hard for some couples—especially if someone they trust said it—but it is so completely necessary to refrain from arguing about "he says, she says." You have to pick and choose your battles and this one just isn't worth it. Trust me.

There's a hundred and one good things to talk about when you're in a relationship like new sex positions to try or how many kids you want in the future. What do ya say we leave these five things out of the picture? Happy chatting!

## 29

# These Things Are Never Worth Fighting About In Your Relationship

Every relationship has it's moments where slapping your partner in the face just seems like an easier alternative than arguing with them. I know all too well that some people are just really good at being petty as hell and those are the types of people that make arguing so tedious. To be honest, if you're in a relationship and the point of the argument isn't the great make-up sex that should follow—why in the hell would you even argue? Nevertheless, here are a few things that are never worth fighting about in your relationship. Let's get into it!

## 1. When someone flirts with your partner.

Listen, your partner has zero control over who thinks they look good. They have even less control over the person who is bold enough to make sure that they know it. Don't take that out on your partner. That is completely unfair. What you can get upset about, however, is your partner's response. Don't be insecure. Let them accept the compliment. Trust that they won't disrespect you or your relationship. Don't make a big deal out of them saying "thank you." That's about all that needs to be said though, I agree with you there.

## 2. Sex, in any way.

Why would you fight about sex when you can have sex? If sex is a cause of an argument it's really because one of you isn't satisfied, which really means that the problem is communication—not sex. If sex seems like a chore to your partner, I can understand how that might be frustrating so I'm not saying that it's never been reason to argue. Instead, try to talk it out and identify the problem so that you can have better sex and eliminate the argument altogether.

## 3. Who spends the money.

The minute you two decide to share funds, now all of a sudden it matters who buys what. No, I don't think you should share funds before marriage, but with the social culture these days a lot of couples do. If you are worried about who spends what then you never should have combined your money in the first place. Establish a plan and follow it. Otherwise, go back to the way things were before you both started sharing.

## 4. When your partner wants to be alone.

It's important that you and your partner get some alone time in. Alone time is different than time spent with separate friends, although that is very important as well. It's completely unfair to be upset with your partner for wanting to have time to themselves. If this is something that triggers an argument for you, it's no wonder they want to get away from you. Try not to overreact or take it personally when your partner tells you they need a little space. If you don't let them go, they can't come back.

## 5. Who does what.

It's important to establish roles within your relationship so that this argument doesn't have the chance to present itself. I hate to hear that a couple is fighting over who should have done something. At the end of the day, I am the kind of person who believes, "if you want something done right, do it yourself." Still, I allow my partner to take responsibility for whatever it is he wants to take care of and I hold him accountable for those things, just as he does for me. We never have to argue about who should have done something because it was already established from the beginning whose responsibility it was.

## 6. Old News

If it happened before you two were together, it has nothing to do with what you two have now. Leave the old shit behind you. PERIOD.

## 7. Old Habits

I think it's very unfair to argue with your partner about habits you knew they had before they got with you. I'm not saying to tolerate any old thing, for example, your partner could have a "habit" of entertaining a lot of people who flirt with them, but that doesn't mean they should do it. What I'm trying to get at here is that you knew they did it before you started them so arguing with them about it seems a bit pointless. You shouldn't be surprised that it's happening. Just remember though, the best apology is changed actions.

## 8. Friends

There's no way you will like every friend your partner has. That doesn't give you the right to suggest who they do and don't associate themselves with. Friends are one of the things I think is off-limits to your partner's opinion. True friends though. I straddle the fence a lot with this, but at the end of the day, a real friend is a real friend whether my partner likes them or not. A real friend would never jeopardize your happiness—or in this case, your relationship, so if they are really your friend you shouldn't have to worry about that.

Make-up sex is amazeballs, but you shouldn't be making up all the time. Learn to let the small shit go.

# 30

# 5 Foolproof Ways To Improve Your Relationship

Getting in a relationship isn't the hard part; staying in that relationship is.

Getting into a relationship is risky—especially when things get "serious." There is no guarantee that this will turn into your happily ever after. Still, the majority of us take that chance—and we should! As long as you're willing to try, I don't see a reason not to embark on a new relationship. When it comes to staying in that relationship though, that's where you may begin to notice how hard being in a successful relationship really can be.

As we hear all the time, a lasting relationship takes work—a LOT of work. I've found that one of the main reasons people end up hitting a hard spot in their relationship so early on in their relationship is because the foundation of the relationship was built on false pretenses. When you're just getting into a relationship, the goal is to impress your partner. Sometimes impressing your partner causes you to start doing things that you might not be able to keep up with later and that is what causes the issue. Then you reach the point of telling your partner about what they used to do for you and vice versa. Rest assured though. No matter how bad things have gotten, no matter how long the two of you have or have not been together, I strongly believe that all is not lost until the both of you decide that you no longer want to try and fix things within your broken relationship. Before things escalate that far and you two no longer feel like your relationship is worth saving, I want to share with you five foolproof ways to improve your relationship. Let's get into it.

## 1. Identify the issue(s) you're having and determine whether or not they can be fixed.

First, you've got to understand that some people just like to argue with you to make sure they can get you worked up. For a lack of better words, some people are just petty. Other times, there really is an issue at hand and it needs to be identified in order for you two to work through it. Once you identify the problem, that will help you both determine whether or not it is something that can be fixed or not. For example, if the problem is in someone's character—that might not be something that can be fixed and if it can, it will definitely take some time. Nevertheless, refrain from holding empty arguments with your partner. Always try to identify the problem first.

## 2. Identify the roles in the relationship.

This is also known as sharing power. You'll be surprised at how quickly things can be resolved when everyone takes responsibility for what they're accountable for. When you identify the roles within your relationship you eliminate a lot of arguments that are a usually the result of "well, I thought you were going to do it."

## 3. Be present in the right now of your relationship.

For the love of God, please don't focus on the past for any reason. Be present in the right now of your relationship. Be thankful for your partner as they are now. Don't date the potential of who they "could" be. Be grateful for what you both have now, don't belittle it because of where you want to be in the future. We really do ourselves a disservice by focusing on what could have been or what should be instead of basking in the moments we are given day-to-day.

## 4. Build a friendship.

When you're focused on the present day of your relationship, you open doors for things that can save your relationship like building a genuine friendship with your partner. When you two are friends, it's a lot easier to stick out the rough times together—and believe me, there will definitely be some rough times. It's also easier to communicate with one another and overall it just makes things better than they were before. While you're basking in the present, build with your partner. Learn them inside and out and really build on the friendship and relationship you two share together.

## 5. Have mutual goals.

Having mutual goals makes you want to work together. It also makes you hold your partner accountable for the things they said they would do for the good of the team (or relationship). When you two have successfully built that bond and nourished your friendship with one another, it is a lot easier to look at life as a team. You will set mutual goals together and honestly, even the individual goals you set will be for the good of your relationship (in most cases).

Every relationship has it's rough times. Some last longer than others, but remember it's worth fighting for if the both of you haven't given up on things. All is certainly not lost until the both of you decide that you no longer want to try and fix things.

# 31

# 7 Things You'll Learn When Shacking Up

"Shacking up," if you haven't heard, is the term older people used when two partners live together without being married. It is a lot more common in our time today than it used to be back then. It was never really looked upon highly then and to be honest, it still isn't looked upon highly by many people now. I've done it a few times, but I think it's a much needed journey to take when you're planning on being with someone for the long run. Not everyone thinks it's a great idea and in fact, plenty of people think it ruins relationships—but as usual...you know I'm always willing to explain my reasons behind my decisions. Here are seven things you'll learn when shacking up. Let's get into it!

## 1. Your clean vs. Their clean

Be mindful that when you're living with someone, you will notice a many more differences than just how clean you or your partner thinks something is, but this is definitely one of the more noticeable differences between you and them. It may be that both of you think it's fine to put dishes in the dishwasher, but one of you may prefer that the dishes are rinsed before putting them in the dishwasher and the other will think it's completely acceptable to just toss 'em in as-is and run the machine.

## 2. Your sex drive vs. Their sex drive

Sex is a huge part of being in a relationship—I think we can all agree on this fact. When you're not living together it may seem that both of your sex drives are high, but that's because you're hungry for one another when you've been away from each other for a while (hopefully). When you're living together though, you'll notice whose sex drive is stronger. It doesn't have to be a deal-breaker or a bad thing, but it is definitely something you'll figure out much sooner than later in the process of shacking up.

## 3. Your tasks vs. Their tasks

This can be very annoying to learn, but when you both get into the swing of things it will be one of those things that can make living together that much better. For example, when I lived with my ex, I wouldn't even waste my breathe asking him to do the laundry—it's just not his thing. AT ALL. At the same time, he knew not to even look my way when it came to doing any type of handy work. If it's not cooking or cleaning or something of that nature…I didn't really look at it as something that needed my undivided attention. I was always willing to help him with his tasks, but he knew that the responsibility was his and his alone to tackle and accomplish. It's a system—and for us, it worked well. It kept us responsible for the individual areas that made our house run smoothly.

## 4. Your side of the bed vs. Their side of the bed

First things first, you'll definitely feel like there is no such thing as 'your side of the bed'. Despite what every person who has never lived with their partner may think…pretty soon that "let's cuddle ourselves to sleep every night" feeling will devour itself. When you live together, it's a whole lot easier to kiss each other goodnight, turn your backs to one another, and whisk away peacefully into a deep sleep. Don't be fooled. Still, there will be those times after a bad day or great sex that cuddling to sleep is 100% necessary, but it's certainly not an every night kind of thing.

## 5. Dealing with your issues at home.

One of the most valuable things I learned when living with my ex was that we were unable to run away from our issues. We made it a point, as cliché as it may sound, not to go to bed mad at one another. When you're not living with your partner, you'll find that it's really easy not to respond to an angry text or to just stay away from your partner while you're angry with them—but when you two are under the same room that's not really an option. You can't put your life in 'airplane mode'. Find value in this. It's actually really good for the longevity of your relationship. You need to be able to face your problems head-on.

## 6. Yours, Mine, OURS.

When you're not living under the same roof, it's very easy

to look at things in the "yours vs. mine" perspective. Beautifully, when the two of you combine your living space, you'll watch the evolution of what once was yours or theirs grow into what belongs to you both. Whether it's wearing their T-shirts as sleep clothes, sharing a bank account or learning to grocery shop for the both of you instead of always fast-fooding things…you'll notice and love the integration of your possessions and lifestyle as a whole.

## 7. Whether or not this is going to work.

Ultimately, you're going to learn your partner in a way you probably never thought imaginable; which—whether or not you like the outcome—is going to show you if this person is the one. This, to me, is the main reason people are scared to make this step and take the relationship to this level of commitment. Sure, some people are honoring their religion or their parents preference, but I think a lot of people are just scared to do it. In my opinion, it's definitely a necessary, but difficult step to make when in a relationship. Most times, one of you will want this more than the other, but every now and then the cosmos align and things end up working out in a way you couldn't believe. You'll see that not too much beats coming home to the person you love, whether you just had the best or worst day of your life.

Shacking up is indeed a challenge, but when you're able to work through the small difficulties, sometimes you can settle into a life that is really comfortable for you both. It doesn't mean that marriage is or isn't in the future, but sometimes you gotta take the car on a test run before you buy it. If you two decide to take this step, please make the best of it—and if you find that it's not for you guys, that is something to be happy about too. Divorce sucks—or so I've heard. So test the waters. Try it out. No judgment here!

# 32

# What He Means When He Says 'I Need Space' (And How To Deal With It)

Honestly, you haven't been happier in any other relationship. You spend the majority of your time with him, thinking about him, or talking about him—it's literally ridiculous how much you love him. The initial first couple of months you two have been together we're damn near perfect, then one day he says it, "Baby, I need some space."

As a woman, this stings—there's no need to deny that. Instantly, we start contemplating what we did wrong that would cause him to need space apart.

We start asking questions like, "Are you thinking about whether or not you want to be with me?" and that honestly just make things worse. Don't get me wrong, I totally understand your concerns, but I've learned from the few times I've been through this that lashing out is the last thing we should do. I think I've finally figured out what we should do instead. Here's how to survive when he says he needs space:

## Acknowledge and respect his request.

Don't argue with him or become upset when he tells you he needs space. For one, there are a lot of men who don't even have the balls to say this. Instead, they just ignore you and expect you to 'take a hint' or 'get the picture.' So do your best to respect the fact that he was man enough to trust you with how he is feeling right now. Also, acknowledge that you understand and care about how he is feeling right now and more importantly that you support his decision—even if your feelings are a little hurt.

## Remember that you're probably not the problem.

Most times, it's not you—it's him. Well, it's not really him either. It's life. We've all had times in our life where shit is just difficult. Unlike women, men don't call their girl friends or their mom and cry or make decisions based on their emotions at the moment. They often take time to think things through, hence their needing space. So, try to understand that he isn't asking for space from you because he doesn't like you anymore (most times), he is asking for space to get his shit together. Let him get his shit together. It will pay off, I promise.

## Remain confident—in all areas.

This is kind of hard to do when your feelings are hurt and your perfect relationship all of sudden isn't so perfect anymore, but you MUST remain confident. Don't let your mind defeat you by making you assume the worst. Stay confident in yourself, stay confident in the strength of your relationship, and stay confident in your partner. You can trust him. The fact that you're even reading this right now proves that you want to give him the space he needs, but you want to make sure you won't lose your baby either. I get it. Just stay confident that you two will make it through this small test.

## Take advantage of the time apart.

Don't sulk. Don't overthink. Don't tell all your friends so that they convince you of anything negative. Take advantage of the space you two are giving each other. Do a few things that make you feel good. Give yourself a makeover so that when you two do see each other you can't resist each other. Learn a new sex trick to spice things up when it's time. Whatever you do, just take advantage of it. Doing this will help you stay positive about the situation and it will make the time go by a hell of a lot faster. Trust me.

## Give him his space.

At the end of the day, you've gotta give the man his space. If you have a good man, don't worry about him doing anything he shouldn't be doing. Remember, all of this is so he can get his shit together—for the both of you. Your relationship will benefit from this in the long run.

As we all know, there is no recipe for the perfect relationship and figuring out the ingredients to a healthy relationship isn't any easier. This might work for you and it might not. It's helping me, that's for sure. Just remember, if in the end he decides that he doesn't want to continue on in the relationship, don't freak out. You'll be all right, girl.

# 33

# 7 Signs You're In Relationship Limbo

It doesn't matter whether it's a romantic relationship or a platonic friendship; a working relationship takes two. No relationship should be forced...period. A lot of the time, we are in denial about the realistic status of a relationship we feel we want and deserve, which is what ultimately leads us into this relationship limbo. The sad part about being in relationship limbo is that one person in the relationship normally cannot tell or does not want to admit that the relationship has gotten to this place. So how do you know if you're relationship is in limbo or not? Here are seven signs of showing you're already there! Let's get into it.

## 1. You only hear from them when you call or text first.

This is a big one and it's usually the first sign of being in relationship limbo. I get it, we've all got busy schedules, but if you only hear from this person on your own motive...something isn't right here. Communication is key. I've learned from personal experiences that it usually starts with your partner expressing a need for personal space and then slowly but surely you begin to hear from them less and less.

## 2. When you do talk to one another, it's never face-to-face communication.

A lot of people have become dependent on expressing themselves through text message instead of actually talking to you face-to-face. When your relationship is heading down hill you might notice that your partner only talks to you through text. When you two are around each other they seem completely distracted and disengaged.

## 3. Conversation seems forced or shortened.

You know what a typical conversation between the two of you sounds like. That means you can notice very quickly when that conversation changes. When the conversation is getting shorter with you, it's usually getting longer with somebody else. When it feels like you're prying when all you're trying to do is ask how their day was, that's not a good sign.

## 4. A lack of quality time.

People make time for what they want to make time for. Even the busiest of people find ways to spend time with the people who are important to them. Remember, quality time doesn't have a limit and doesn't have to occur at a certain place in order to be deemed valuable. It's about the generosity of the visit and the time you both get to spend together. No matter how long or short.

## 5. You only hear from them when they need or want something.

Most times you're so caught up in being loyal to the relationship that you don't even realize you're being used in this manner. If you care about this person you'll find it hard to say no to them when they are in a time of need, but you need to be able to. If they only time you hear from this person from their own initiative is because they need something, again…things are not looking to bright for the future.

## 6. A lack of affection.

If affection and appreciation are not vivid, that's already a red flag right there. Although you should hear that you mean something to this person, you should absolutely feel it. If you two can't sit and cuddle or sit and talk, or sit and cuddle while you talk…there is definitely an issue at hand. If being intimate with you in any way feels like a chore for them, then that is a major sign that they are not into anything you two have going on anymore. Showing affection shouldn't be hard and it most definitely shouldn't be forced.

## 7. You feel most appreciated when you're having sex.

That's right. If you feel like the most "magical" time in the relationship is during sex or the five minutes you spend cuddled up after sex… chances are there is no real connection between you two. Yes, this goes for "friends with benefits" relationships as well.

Never be afraid to evaluate the need for the relationships and friendships you're in. It takes two to be in a functioning relationship, no matter what the type. Don't hold onto false pretenses and don't be in denial about how genuine someone is being with you. Your heart is no toy and your time is valuable. Act like you know this. Don't be afraid to do a little 'spring cleaning' in your relationship closet this season. Know when it's time to move on!

## 34

# How To Apologize When You (Really) Fucked Up

Okay, before we get into things, let us first acknowledge that nobody is perfect. I get that. However, that is not a good enough reason to neglect knowing how to apologize to someone when you've done something wrong. It doesn't mean you cheated, it could simply be a time that you didn't show them support when they needed it most. Either way, the key to any lasting relationship is forgiveness—but it's kind of hard to forgive someone who didn't even apologize for their wrongful actions to begin with. When I came up with this topic, I sat and thought of real-life examples in my own life. Whether I needed to apologize or I needed the apology from someone, I found that the death of most of those relationships was simply in the failure to apologize. Most times, when you apologize to someone and mean it, the two of you are able to push forward and continue pursuing a healthy relationship. As I always remind you, do not limit the term 'relationship' to just one type of relationship—these things go for platonic relationships, social relationships, and family relationships as well. I'm not saying that all mistakes can be made right simply by apologizing, but there's no harm in trying. So, if you've ever needed to know how to apologize when you've really messed up, here are five steps to doing just that. Let's get into it!

## Seek advice from a trusted source.

I believe in getting a (trusted) second opinion in just about everything—so in my case, if I'm feeling guilty or like I've done something wrong to someone, I tell a trusted source about it. I do this for a number of different reasons, but ultimately it's so that I have an opportunity to openly express myself without fear of being judged. When we do things we end up having to apologize for, the motive is not always simply to hurt someone. Sometimes we do it from anger, sorrow, and a heap of other emotions. When you confide in someone you trust, you have a chance to really let out all of your emotions behind why you made the choice you did.

Outside of that, the other most important reason I seek the advice of someone else is because I don't have all the answers. The way that I might think it's appropriate to apologize could be completely wrong. Or I could do one of the worst things possible, not seek a second opinion and end up convincing myself that I don't need apologize at all.

## Accept and admit your fault.

Hopefully, you see the importance in confiding in someone you trust about what has happened. Hopefully, they supported you and encouraged you to apologize to the person you hurt. The first thing to do after getting trusted advice is to accept the hurt you've caused the other person involved and to immediately apologize to them. Remember, you should

ALWAYS APOLOGIZE IN PERSON if you are physically capable of doing so.

No, none of us like admitting that we are wrong, but this is a very important step in order for the other person to be able to forgive you. Admitting what you did wrong will show the other person involved that you are aware of exactly the actions that caused them the hurt they are feeling. Although it sucks for you, they deserve to know that you understand the measures of your specific actions.

## Verbally and visibly show empathy and remorse.

Some people say that saying, "I'm sorry," doesn't mean anything, but that isn't necessarily true. Just saying, "I'm sorry," isn't all that matters when apologizing, but still it's a piece of the puzzle. You've got to pay a price for your actions and they deserve to feel good about what you're doing. This step is supposed to support the both of you in feeling confident that the apology is, indeed, a sincere one.

Verbally showing empathy and remorse means to tell that person that you understand how bad your actions hurt them (and it wouldn't be a horrible idea to share the reasons why you care about them so much in the first place). Visibly showing empathy and remorse leaves you room for creativity, but is highly encouraged so that you let the person you hurt know you mean what you're saying. Some people like to receive gifts like flowers, while others would really appreciate a written letter of affection. Hone in on what the person you're apologizing to would consider a thoughtful gesture and offer that to them as a token of your remorse, as well.

## Present a solution they can trust.

When I was younger I was told never to present a problem without a solution—you may have heard that before. I don't think that this is only applicable in school, work, or business. I *live* by it. Come up with a plan that will allow the person you're apologizing to to confidently take your word when you promise them you won't do this again. It doesn't have to be elaborately drawn out, but it should be true and trustworthy. Yes, that means deleting trails of temptation (i.e., telephone numbers, followers, and the means for any other temptation you may have) and eliminating other sources that caused the problem in the first place. You've got to show them that you mean it when you say it won't happen again. If this step is hard for you, think of how you would feel if whatever it is you did to them, happened to you. Let that (probably shitty) feeling motivate you to follow through with this step.

## Don't fuck up again.

Plain and simple. Don't go through all of this only to repeat the "same mistake" again. You absolutely deserve what's coming to you if you do. That's just my personal opinion. If you find that you're still falling short of your promises and leaning toward whatever tempted you to get in the position you were in initially, remove yourself from the relationship so that you're not hurting that person again. It sucks to have the same wound opened twice. Trust me.

I hope these steps help. You don't have to follow them word for word or in order, but based on my personal experiences…they work.

# 35

# 5 Obvious Signs You're With The Wrong Person

As if finding the right one isn't already hard enough, here I am telling you that after you've finally found someone, they may not be the right person for you. I'm such an asshole. It's honest though. The best pieces of advice are usually like a shot of whiskey—a little hard to swallow, but always good to the soul. Here are five obvious signs you're with the wrong person. Let's get into it.

## 1. You compare them to your ex.

You shouldn't even be in a new relationship if you haven't had closure from your past relationship(s). If you are comparing the things your current partner does or doesn't do with that of your ex, you're definitely not with the right person. In fact, that's a huge sign that you're not even over your ex.

## 2. You have a long list of improvements for them.

I called off my engagement because an elder asked me one simple question—"If he never changed, would you still want to spend the rest of your life with him?" The truth of the matter was if he didn't make the changes that I wanted him to make, he wouldn't ever be good enough for me. Most people won't admit this, but for a long time I only dated men I needed to "fix." I never saw that as a bad thing. I liked projects, not realizing that those relationships failed effortlessly every single time.

## 3. You don't feel the need to improve yourself.

As I said before, I liked projects. They made me feel good about myself. Don't get me wrong—I'm an amazing girlfriend, but we can all do a little better in some area. I never felt like I needed to improve myself, only the man I was with at the time. When I met my current partner, he put such a driving force in me to be better in just about every area of my life. He didn't verbally tell me I needed to improve anything either. He was just that good to me that I wanted to be better for him. That's the way it should be, in my opinion.

## 4. Your close friends and family don't like them.

Period, point blank. No, you don't need to take everyone's opinion about him to heart. Some people won't like them because they feel like they're being replaced and for other selfish reasons. However, if practically everyone who is close to you has a problem with this individual—especially your parents or sibling(s)—you're not with the right person.

## 5. You're not excited or concerned about a future with them.

You feel like you're going to be just fine with or without them. A lot of people like to justify this by saying that they are in charge of their own happiness, which I completely agree with. However, that doesn't mean that your life partner (or partner for the time being) isn't supposed to contribute in large part to that happiness. If you don't feel like you need them (no, not financially) or desire to have a future with them, then move on. You deserve to be with someone who makes you feel the way you do when you see your food coming to your table in a restaurant.

If you're holding on to someone that you know isn't right for you, do yourself the favor and let go of them. Don't sell yourself short. The right one is out there somewhere.

## 36

# 10 Reasons To Be Thankful For A Broken Heart

Getting your heart broken sucks monkey balls.

Very few people can honestly say they haven't gotten their heart broken at least one time. I'd like to think mine has been broken more times than one hand will let me show, but ehh, you work through it. Although it doesn't feel good and it's hard to see any good from it, there are a lot of benefits to having a broken heart and even more when you heal from it. Here are ten reasons to be thankful for a broken heart.

## 1. You no longer have to waste your time.

If it isn't the real thing, then it isn't the right thing. It doesn't matter how much you thought it was or how badly you wanted things to work. When things went bad and your heart was broken, it did you one favor you probably didn't realize. It stopped you from wasting any more time on a relationship that wasn't ever going to give you the happy ending you deserve.

## 2. Your friends and family show you just how much they love you.

You're going to be hurt initially. Heartbreak isn't an easy thing to overcome and although you might feel really alone while you're healing, the people who love you notice how hurt you are. Seeing you in pain, even if it is emotional, gives your friends and family all the more reason to remind you of how important you are to them. If you don't have any friends or family that came to your rescue when your heart was broken, I'd reevaluate some of those relationships.

## 3. You can now call bullshit as soon as you see it coming.

No playboys will be able to pull the wool over your eyes again. At this point, you can smell the bullshit from a mile away. You do have to be careful not to compare your next guy with the guy who broke your heart, but be cautious too. It won't always look or sound the same, but you can tell a little better from now on when someone is trying to play you.

## 4. You see how much of a badass you are for yourself.

Say it with me: *I am a pink Starburst.* You are the shit. When you overcome heartbreak you get the opportunity to see yourself for the badass you really are. It's easy to think that the weak, pained woman we become during the heartbreak is really who we are, but don't fool yourself. That's not you! You can and will handle this.

## 5. You're stronger than you were before.

All of a sudden things that used to hurt your feelings just don't anymore. You're so much stronger than you used to be because if you can overcome the pain of heartbreak, there isn't too much more you can't handle! When you realize how much of a badass you are, that confidence also allows you (and everyone else) to see how much stronger you've become from this.

## 6. You're no longer afraid of being alone.

At first, this will seem like the biggest lie, but it's not. When you start working through the heartbreak you'll see that spending time alone doesn't mean you have to spend it sulking or moping around. You can spend quality time with yourself. Get to know yourself better. Start talking to that badass you found out about and make sure the next time you leave the house that she'll be with you.

## 7. You're patient about getting back out there.

Having your heart broken will make you feel very hesitant about finding love again, but you should promise yourself that with time, you will. You let the heartbreaker win when you decide not to get back out there. You can't think that the same thing will happen twice. Although, it can—you shouldn't get back out there with that thought already consuming your mind. Take your time. Trust your gut. Get back out there.

## 8. You have a better idea of what you want.

When you take the time to learn the confident version of you and you start spending more quality time with yourself, you're bound to learn what you're looking for is pretty different from what you had the first time around. Having your heart broken is usually a huge help in determining what we do and don't want in the next relationship.

## 9. You'll appreciate your next relationship so much more.

You took your time getting to know yourself. You took your time getting back out into the dating game. You took the time to better identify what you want. Now, you've met him. You will appreciate your next partner so much more than your last one because (hopefully) you've worked through all the pain your heartbreak caused you and you can now embrace your new relationship head-on.

## 10. You got a chance to try love.

As optimistic as I am about you getting back out there, it isn't always easy for everyone. What I want to make sure that you don't do is harbor hate for the person who broke your heart.

At one point, you loved that person with all that you were. Try to remember that version of them. People are stupid. Chances are they didn't mean to hurt you. No, that doesn't change the fact that they did, but you never would have danced with love if it weren't for your meeting them.

Try to remember that the best is yet to come. Protect your heart, but get out there and find who you're looking for.

# 37

# 4 Things You Get Better At Every Time You Get Cheated On

You probably think you read the title wrong, but you didn't. There are plenty benefits to getting cheated on should you choose to look at it that way. I completely understand that in the heat of the moment, you're not so keen on looking at this way though. Never you fear. After reading this you probably won't even view cheating as a bad thing—okay, that's a lie, but you definitely won't feel like all is lost if you ever get cheated on again. Here are four things you get better at every time you get cheated on. Let's get into it.

## 1. You learn how to reciprocate actions without giving "too" much.

I used to be an over-doer. I used to outdo myself every time I did something for my partner. At the time, it didn't seem tedious or stupid. It wasn't until I got cheated on the first time that I ever even felt like it wasn't a good thing. I wasn't really mad about the fact that I got cheated on. I was pissed off at all that I had done for him and still it wasn't enough to encourage him to be faithful and keep his dick in his pants.

## 2. You learn not to let one bad apple spoil the rest of the bunch.

So, you fell for a douche? It's okay. You took one for the team. At least you can warn others about them. It doesn't mean that everyone else you meet will cheat on you like they did. Honestly, that's a very childish way of thinking. You'll get a lot better at separating one bad apple from the rest of the bunch. Don't fool yourself, some people really do want the "real thing."

## 3. You learn how to spot a cheater.

Although all the apples aren't bad, you'll be able to spot any other bad apples when you see them. It won't be rocket science trying to figure out whether or not someone else is running serious game on you. Try to pay close attention to any signs that you saw this time around so that you can avoid them within any other relationship you pursue. At the end of the day, the more you get played, the easier it'll be to see them before they get you. Simple as that.

## 4. You learn that you really are the shit.

Getting cheated on is the perfect reason to go and do whatever crazy makeover thing you've been contemplating. Men, you probably don't have one of these, but I know the majority of the women reading this right now, do. Cut your hair. Dye your hair. Go buy that dress that made your boobs look great because when you get cheated on you deserve to remind yourself that you really are the shit. It's their loss, not yours. Stroke your ego for as long as you need to. Seeing as how I've been cheated on more than once, I am always able to make my little changes bolder every time. I unapologetically let my bad-assedness show.

## 38

# 10 Signs You're Not Over Your Ex (No Matter How Much You Want To Be)

If you're still sleeping with them, you shouldn't need to read anything else to know that you're definitely not over your ex.

However, there are some things that we do when it comes to our exes that indicate we aren't as over them as we believe ourselves to be. The thing is, we just don't realize it right away. Here are 10 signs you're definitely not over your ex. Let's get into it!

### 1. You cyber-stalk them daily.

You know exactly what I'm talking about. They are the first name in your recent searches on all of your social media platforms. You don't check in on them though. You never reach out to them, but you keep up with their every move—or post.

### 2. You speak badly about them.

I can't stand to hear someone speak badly about their ex. Yes, even if they cheated. At one point, that person was everything to you and bad mouthing them only reflects on you and your choice of partner. To be frank, it makes you look bad.

## 3. You aren't happy that they're happy.

If you see that they get into a new relationship, you're not happy for them. In most cases, you say that their new partner isn't attractive or you find another way to make them look like less of a person than you are. Shallow!

## 4. You don't like to hear their name.

You can't even stand the sound of their name without getting sad or upset. Just hearing their name brings memories rushing into your mind and in turn, triggers your rash emotions.

## 5. You've disassociated yourself from the people you knew in common.

You're unable to associate yourself with his family and friends. Most times, the people we meet through our ex will only preserve the memories you two shared together and remind you of them when they see you. If you're not over your ex, this is hard to overcome. When you are over your ex, you don't have any problem talking to or being around those people.

## 6. You're not open to new relationship opportunities.

You're completely turned off by the thought of another relationship. You ignore the people who hit on you. Some might argue, but I think holding yourself back from the opportunity to date again is a way of saying,"I'll wait a little longer… just in case they come back."

## 7. You compare the potential of a new relationship to the one you were in with them.

Not only are you not open to talking to that beautiful person who hit on you earlier, but you're bitter and negative about the thought of a new relationship simply based on the results of your last one. Every chance you get, you justify your reasons for why you won't get into anything new by comparing it to things that happened with your ex.

## 8. You're still holding onto relationship memorabilia.

I truly believe that the greatest memories are kept in the heart. If you can't part with the tangible items, you're probably not over them.

## 9. You constantly verbalize that you're over them.

The only person who believes you when you say that you're over your ex is you. If you were really over your ex, your actions would say that for you. No one would question it and you definitely wouldn't have to tell anybody that you're over them.

## 10. You can't see yourself being friends with them—ever.

Being friends with your ex is not a bad thing. In fact, when you're truly over your ex, it's a good thing to be friends with them. If you cannot fathom being friends with your ex at all, it's safe to say that your heart is still healing. If they still bring about ill feelings for you, your heart has not yet coped with the fact that you two aren't together anymore.

If you're experiencing any of the above signs, just give it time. You can get over them. It'll take some time, but I promise you it's possible. Hang in there!

# 39

# 10 Mature Reasons To Be Friends With Your Ex

In order to successfully be friends with your exes, it's important that you understand that you can NEVER have sex with them again and that both of you would have to mature and emotionally stable enough to develop an actual friendship with each other. When you two are able to do those things, being friends with your ex is a walk in the park. Although many people would tell you not to, I've got ten mature reasons to be friends with your ex. Let's get into it!

## 1. Being friends is easier than being enemies.

I don't know about you, but it takes me a lot of energy to be angry with someone. I'd assume that being enemies is even harder than that. To be frank, I just don't have time for it. I am not friends with all my exes, so I'm not saying that this can happen with all of them—but instead of hating the ones I can't befriend, I simply relieve myself of the memory. Friends or forgotten…those are pretty much your only options.

## 2. You have mutual friends.

When you two were a couple, you made friends that neither

of you should have to part with simply because you aren't dating anymore. If you're able to be friends with your ex you won't have to lose any of the friends that you guys made together. Don't put your friends in the position to have to choose between you and your ex. It's unfair and unnecessary.

## 3. You're mature enough to handle it.

What other reason do you need? You're definitely mature enough to be cordial with your ex. No pressure.

## 4. You made memories together.

Even though things didn't work out between you two, the time you shared together was special. You made memories that shouldn't be tainted because you two are harboring ill feelings for one another. When you're able to be friends with your ex you don't have to try and forget memories that really aren't all that easy to get rid of in the first place.

## 5. You have to see each other anyway.

Maybe you live in a big city where you see tons of new people every day, but for the most of us that isn't the case. With having mutual friends and living in the same city, you're bound to see each other at some point. If your friends with your ex, this encounter doesn't have to be a nasty one. Instead you might even find yourself happy to see them! Imagine that.

## 6. Your family has established a relationship with him/her.

The worst part about ending things badly with an ex for me is having to break up with their family, too. I literally hate having to do this, which is another reason I un-learned that you can't be friends with your ex. When things are serious with you and your partner, you (usually) build close relationships with the members of their family, just like with your mutual friends, you shouldn't put your family in the position to have to "break up" with your ex just because you can't handle seeing them.

## 7. You know too much about each other.

At the end of the day, you two know way too much about one another to hate each other. Shit can get ugly. You don't want those problems. You don't have to be worried about what your ex might expose about you if you two are friends. Honestly, just give yourself the security. Let's face it, we all have exes that just know too much.

## 8. You can establish a genuine friendship with one another.

Sometimes when you're in a relationship, you don't get the opportunity to really build a genuine friendship with your partner. Not because you don't want to, but because not every-body is capable of building multiple types of relationships at once. When you two are no longer involved romantically, you gain the opportunity to truly establish a genuine friendship. Take advantage of that.

## 9. You love them.

Let's face the facts. You may not be in love with them, but you love them. You care about their well-being. You share firsts, memories, and friends. Don't be stubborn and don't lie to yourself about that. There is nothing wrong with acknowledging this. In fact, if you're truly over them it's even easier to accept this.

## 10. You don't know what the future holds.

I'll say it if you won't. No one knows what the future holds, so really and truly this may or may not be the end for you two. Only time will tell. Your ex might not have to be "the one who got away" later on in your life. Instead they may just be "the one who got away"…for now.

# 40

# 5 Things You Need To Remember When You're Feeling Really Fucking Lonely

If you're reading this right now, I'm guessing you've been feeling a little lonely. That's nothing to be ashamed of. It's nothing to jump for joy about, either, but still it's a normal emotion and we all feel that way sometimes. Loneliness can really have an emotional toll on you if you allow it to and that's what I'd like to avoid for the both of us. When loneliness sneaks up on me, there are five things I always have to remind myself of in order to get and keep myself out of the mindset that "nobody loves me." Let's get into it!

## 1. You're overlooking the people who do care about you.

Unfortunately, I have to remind myself of the plenty of people who do make me feel loved and appreciated on a regular basis. Sometimes, when we're looking for that "special" feeling from a special someone, we forget about the other people in our life that give us that same feeling, just in a different way. Be careful of overlooking those people because their love is just as important as that of a significant other's love. Sure, it feels a bit different, but it's necessary and you need it. Don't forget that.

## 2. Everything looks better on Instagram.

From celebrity couples to friends from high school, looking at other couples on social media is sure to lead you down the path of loneliness. Avoid doing this at all cost. I know you feel like you're strong enough to handle it and to be honest, that is completely beside the point. The reason I want you to avoid looking at other couples on social media is because it's not real life. Everything looks better on Instagram. Whatever couple you think is absolutely perfect and "just what you deserve" normally is nothing like what you see online. Keep your personal goals and fantasies and feed off of those things. Comparison won't lead you anywhere special, trust me.

## 3. You're never really as lonely as you think you are.

I usually feel the loneliest after watching a love story or seeing a couple online (like I just told you not to do), which is exactly why I suggest avoiding that. No matter how lonely we feel, we usually aren't as lonely as we're letting on. Again, don't overlook those people who are there for you. Also, remember that sometimes that special person is already a part of our life, but we have them stuck in the friend zone where they don't belong. Keep people in your life that make you feel happy and appreciated. Always. Be sure to trim the fat (the people who don't make you feel happy and appreciated) as well. They are a cause of loneliness as well.

## 4. Even loneliness feels better than wasting time on a person who isn't deserving of it.

This is a big one. Even though feeling lonely sucks monkey balls, nothing feels worse than giving yourself and your time to someone who doesn't deserve it. Don't waste time with anyone who doesn't deserve your undivided love and attention just to cope with temporary loneliness. Avoid this at all costs. No one-night stands, booty calls, or trips back to ex-town, people. Seriously. No matter how satisfying it feels at that moment, it is sure to feel ten times worse when you're left feeling just as lonely as you did before that encounter.

## 5. Your happy ending is coming.

This is the most important reminder, of course. Always remember that happiness is in your future. It might not look or feel even remotely close to what you expect, but it's coming if you're willing to accept it. In the meantime, focus on the relationship with yourself and your loved ones. It's hard to focus on loneliness when you center yourself in love. Trust me on this.

# About the Author

Isis Nezbeth is a fresh, free-spirited freelance writer and author. She is a proud twenty-something Scorpio woman who is dedicated to living freely and fulfilling her destiny in life. She just recently added MILF to her resume thanks to her beautiful daughter, Harper. Her passions include writing, spreading joy, and making love.

Isis is a hopeless romantic who still believes in true love at all costs. She enjoys pursuing relationships and although she hasn't stumbled upon the real thing just yet, she won't stop trying and writing about it until she gets there.

Her end goal is to write enough to make at least three people change their life, to make a thousand people smile, and to some day afford a city view with the luxury of keeping her brandy in a decanter on the mantel.

Connect with Isis on thegoddesscolumn.com.

## Thought Catalog, it's a website.

www.ingramcontent.com/pod-product-compliance
Lightning Source LLC
Chambersburg PA
CBHW022334280326
41934CB00006B/629